DATE DUE			
Mar 27 '83			
Apr 27 '83			

ONTOLOGY OF HUMOR

ONTOLOGY
OF
HUMOR

by
THE REV. DR. BOB W. PARROTT

PHILOSOPHICAL LIBRARY
New York

808.701
P240
121430
June 1982

Library of Congress Cataloging in Publication Data

Parrott, Bob W.
    Ontology of humor.

    1. Wit and humor—Philosophy.   2. Religion and humor.
I. Title.
PN6149.P5P27   808.7'01   81-80239
ISBN 0-8022-2387-7   AACR2

Copyright 1982 by Philosophical Library, Inc.
200 West 57 Street, New York, N.Y. 10019

Manufactured in the United States of America

Overseas distributor: George Prior Ltd.
37-41 Bedford Row, London WC1R 4JH, England.

TO

THE COSMIC IRONIST, BEING-ITSELF

FOREWORD

As I have read, thoughtfully and with enjoyment, Dr. Bob W. Parrott's significant book, "Ontology of Humor," my mind has repeatedly turned to an old friend, H. B. Andrews.

This may appear to be an odd reaction, for Mr. Andrews' total formal education encompassed only the first three grades of school. But he became one of the leading businessmen of Syracuse, New York. He was an extraordinary man. He invented the dishwasher, operated the first supermarket in the United States and had a wide reputation as a wise and perceptive layman. He was truly a self-made scholar—a man of learning.

He explained his "wisdom" and in-depth insights into the reality of existence simply by saying that he "went to school to the Bible, the greatest university and library of books."

He would not have been familiar with the professional terminology used in this book, but with his keen mind and spiritually sharpened mental perceptiveness, Mr. Andrews profoundly comprehended the nature of existence or being. To him all being was spiritually conceived, all existence designed with perfection, since it was created by God, the Perfect Being. Yet he saw and genuinely appreciated the incongruities in human existence. "God cannot be understood without recognizing his sense of humor," he would say. His Bible was interlined with his own characteristic comments. "Ha Ha" he would write on the margin where a sinner was described as experiencing his just desserts. "Ha Ha," said Brother Andrews (as he was called), "this fellow got what was coming to him."

Always the greatest saints I have known have practiced a religion that had a deep and joyous laugh in it. The joy emanated from their experience of victory through spiritually changed life and eventuated, inevitably, in an urbane, philosophical understanding of incongruity. They have known firsthand "The Ontology of Humor," though undoubtedly would not have been able to designate it as such.

This succinct, yet comprehensive, book may very well become a classic in Christian literature and make a significant contribution to contemporary theology in its definitive expression of humor as an inherent factor in faith. The committed and literate Christian knows that joy is basic in Christianity. "And these things write we unto you, that your joy may be full" (1 John 1:4); and, "Rejoice in the Lord alway; and again I say Rejoice" (Philippians 4:4). The humor, even the fun, despite this hard life, tends to bubble out of the believer. But the long shadow of his puritanical inheritance still, to some degree, falls athwart his Christian experience, bringing with it a sense of guilt for equating God to any extent with humor. It still seems more proper to be a bit of a sobersides about one's religion, though the "Praise the Lord" psychology is gaining wider acceptance.

This book should mark a milestone in that it will give a more scientific credibility, in a theological and philosophical sense, to humor as an essential spiritual concomitant of being. This variation in Christian thinking should ultimately result in a feeling that the Divine Being, while no less mysterious and sublime, is perhaps an even more loveable Heavenly Father.

Years ago there was on the American platform a famous humorist, Strickland Gilliland, a sort of Bob Hope of his day. I heard him in a lecture on the nature and philosophy of humor in the course of which he said something like the following: "We have a very adroit God who, having put the element of adversity into his creation of man, balanced it with humor in his nature so that he might endure it." This insight into the nature of humanity seems to be emphasized by Dr. Parrott. Nevertheless, I am impressed by the potential impact upon every-day Christians of the work of professional thinkers.

This book deserves a wide reading for it deals expertly with vital concerns. Bob Parrott is himself a happy and delightful synthesis of the preeminent scientific scholar and the down-to-earth, loveable pastor. This fact comes through to add charm to an important work, "The Ontology of Humor."

NORMAN VINCENT PEALE

CONTENTS

PREFACE

This volume produces a double challenge for the philosopher/theologian. He/she must be evaluative while unraveling the ontology and open to humor at the same time. The evaluative reading can be looked at up close. The humor in a writing is seen at a distance. For instance, it was not funny the night that I had a cold. Felt bad. My wife brought a warm piece of cherry pie à la mode and placed it on the flat arm of the big easy chair. I proceeded to knock the pie onto the floor. She said, "Let me clean it up." I said, "I'll do it." On my hurried way down to get to the splattered cherries swimming in an ocean of vanilla ice cream, I bumped her elbow, and her pie finished decorating the floor with the most colorful gunk I ever saw. No matter how reasonable I tried to be, it was not a laughing matter. It is now.

If the philosopher/theologian reads this book from the musing perspective of how the loss of pie and ice cream would affect a starving world, or if he/she asks whether ice cream remains ice cream after it is melted, or whether a pie is a pie when it is splashed across the floor, he/she will never get *it*. I personally have a problem in believing that these kinds of thinkers are philosophers or theologians. They sound more like frozen brains that have yet to thaw out. I hope this book will have a thawing effect for that type of thinker, and permit him/her to become a good-humored human who likes to think about it.

Some philosophers/theologians feel that they must play it "straight," and never give in to being in good humor. This book has a good word for that person. If that one is not laughing, somebody else is. No one is funnier than the one who thinks he/she is the most serious thinker in the world. To the world this problem solver looks too much like the problem!

No one is funnier than he/she who thinks he/she is and has to explain his/her jokes to prove it. But not funny in the way they think. I once had a sociology professor in college who was plagued by this method. He knew he had a rich sense of humor tempered by shrewdness. He knew he was a funny man and felt compelled to help others see it. He would tell a joke and start laughing. The students would start smiling at his laughing. Then when he would stop laughing and explain the joke, the students stopped smiling and got as serious as he in trying to understand the joke. "Get it?" he would ask. That was the cue to "heh heh." The professor knew that he was amply equipped with humor. To him he lacked an audience with sense enough to laugh when he performed. He very nearly worked himself to death trying to get the joke understood.

This book takes humor seriously. It provides the philosopher/theologian insights without explanations, thought experiences without manipulation, a feel for the humorous without trying to be funny. The academic dimension of this writing will have been accomplished if these provisions have been communicated. I hope that academicians in other fields of learning will read this volume and find an appreciation for the philosopher/theologian who not only can have a sense of humor but can help them see humor in themselves, help them become philosophical in humor about who they are in the roles they play.

Finally, deep down everybody with any thinking sense at all feels he/she is a bit of philosopher. For that person this book is written. If one paragraph triggers an insight into humor, it will have been worth the reading. On another day with another reading maybe another insight will come. A reading like this will be in keeping with the way the book was written—over a period of six years, one insight at a time.

My thanks to God Who made this writing possible; Who gave to me a personal awareness of His Being-itself; Who permitted me to know in His absence a consciousness of nothingness, to know non-being. Some would call this writing abstract. I would not. This awareness of Being-itself and non-being holds together with meaning what we call the "concrete." Ontology *is* the concrete.

Psalm 2:4 says: "He who sits in the heavens laughs." This ontology shows that God does not laugh alone. That He shares His laugh with us. That we can have a sense of humor with Him who makes humor possible.

My thanks to the many authors whose writings triggered cosmic thoughts on the subject, and made the final writing a kind of co-venture of many with the Cosmic Ironist, Being-itself.

My thanks to Dr. Herndon Wagers, Dr. William Power, and Dr. Albert C. Outler, whose contributions in dialogue were invaluable. Especially do I owe a debt of gratitude to Dr. Leroy Howe, who chaired my doctoral committee on the thesis "Biblical Preaching and the Use of Humor." He asked me to write an essay for the *Perkins Journal* on "Ontology of Humor, a Basis for Biblical Exegesis." His abilities to maneuver in metaphysics gave him editing capabilities that make this academic writing readable to the inquiring mind.

My thanks to my secretary, Ms. Eloise Wilson, who has shown tireless devotion to this project in typing, editing and retyping.

And finally to my wife, Doris, who has witnessed first-hand the evolution of this project through the years, who has seen tears turn to laughter in her author-husband, and who has in her own ways helped him not take himself too seriously in the quest.

Part I

HUMOR IS AN ONTOLOGICAL PROBLEM

As a whole, published books on wit and humor scout around in concrete areas. Specific areas. Specific examples, such as satire and irony, have been explored thoroughly.[1] This book is essentially abstract, illustrated by concrete examples.

The purpose of this book is to show that an ontological examination of humor can bring relief to the theologian/philosopher who finds himself/herself stereotyped as a "square." Hopefully this treatise will permit humor to come alive in the philosopher to the extent that he/she can laugh at himself/herself and let the world see the humor. Humor is inherently a part of the finite makeup of men and women. Indeed, they are human *being* in their playful humor. I would like to see the theologian/philosopher become by his/her own self-understanding a part of that humorous condition.

Some authors admit humor is an ontological problem.

> The humorist is a laughing philosopher out of this world, who sees bits of nonsense in a world that somehow makes sense, who grasps incongruities in a more comprehensive congruity. . . . Metaphysically, we would suggest, the very presupposition of the possibility of taking an impartial, objective attitude in judging the ludicrous involves an ontological structure. . . . If we are right, the perception of the comic, besides involving emotional and

1

physiological response, requires logical and metaphysical comprehension, a normative intellectual insight which grasps what is worthy of what makes us as organic creatures laugh.[2]

I found no author who attempted to elaborate the metaphysical problem of humor. In the initial part of the book, ontological categories are used to point to the function of humor within the human situation. Ontological categories are defined as covering all expressions of being—from Being-itself to a human *being* in all of the ways that a human *is*. We refer to the physiological or the psychological categories insofar as what they say *is*; when they do that, they give expression to the ontic, an ontological category belonging to the finite. Ontology brings together the essential and the actual and offers a transcending form of reference for the finite and the infinite.

A. *Humor Belongs on Earth*

I. *Humor is a finite experience.* Humor in finitude shows that playful laughter is unself-consciously good for the soul. Max Eastman describes the finite human being in playful humor in this manner:

> It seems to me just here that nature, in her necessity to make us happy when we play—by what interior means we can hardly guess—has triumphed over the very terms of life. For she has ordained it in the inmost structure of our minds that playful dreadfulness instead of hurting makes us laugh. Indeed it is the first sure sign of play in babies when they giggle instead of looking troubled at our gargoyle faces, and when they find amusement in our snatching away a thing they have reached out to grasp. That feeling of amusement is a new, unique one, and that giggle is a different act from the smile of gratification which greets a friendly look. It is an act of welcoming a playful shock or disappointment. . . . It is an instinct. And this instinct is the germ and simple rudiment of what we call the sense of humor. . . . That humorous laughter belongs among the hereditary instincts

2

is indicated by the fact that it appears so early and so spontaneously. We never have to teach children when to laugh; we have to teach them when not to laugh.[3]

Humor is meaningful because by means of it one is able to cope positively with what otherwise could be a completely baffling experience. When the sudden incongruity arises, when what was (now you see it) is not any longer (now you abruptly do not see it), laughter conquers the existential anxiety (rather, it permits us to live with the anxiety). The humor nature remains a redemptive aspect of the finite human situation. It helps us deal with the surprising, the different, with the unexpected in finitude.

2. *The humor context broadens with sin-in-finitude.* Dante, in his *Divine Comedy*, without attempting to come off as a joke-telling comic, points to the sinful human situation in which the humorous comes alive. Heaven, lacking incongruities, needs no laughter in the earthly sense. Joy accompanies that complete sense of well-being. Any laughter there would be an expression of joy rather than of incongruities. Ultimate sublimity of being with God fulfills the self's needs. "Life is sublime in every realm dominated by the dimension of the spirit."[4] In hell no one *can* laugh (or cry in the earthly sense; crying would imply that there is something unfulfilled to cry about). Hell might be termed the leavings of man's sin on earth. Dante describes the tragedy of hell, where he saw history's greatest teachers—Plato, Socrates, Democritus, Hippocrates, to name a few. The teachers who showed others the way to go had no place to go themselves. Those who felt they "had it all" had nothing. They possessed on earth forms for truth; but no forms of truth possessed them!

Dante pictured the lovers who died together because they loved too much themselves. Sometimes when we say, "I love you," we are really saying, "I love myself." For instance, it is easier to say, "I love you," to a wife who cooks warm meals than to say, "I love you," to her as you come face to face with an old cold potato.

Dante shows that the perfectionist, who may be perfect in

3

every aspect of his life, by his very nature lacks patience with himself and others and renders himself the most imperfect of all. He sees those who strive for fame and fortune and goodness as finally robbing the soul of its rest, of the very comfort it seeks. Hell lurks behind the shadows of this existence as the dead results of pride (self-centred *hubris*).

> *Hubris* is the self-elevation of man into the sphere of the divine. . . . People have identified their limited goodness with absolute goodness . . . man identifies his cultural creativity with divine creativity. He attributes infinite significance to his finite cultural creations, making idols of them, elevating them into matters of ultimate concern.[5]

Self-centered *hubris* here on earth results in a death described this way by Dante:

> I am Oberto, and my *pride* does harm
> Not to myself alone, for all my kin
> Were dragged thereby down to calamity.
> And 'tis for it that I must bear this
>   burden
> Here mid the dead, till God be satisfied.
> For mid the living, I endured it not.[6]

In non-being ("mid the dead") one bears the burden of pride. A thorough look at pride, at what it finally amounts to, brings an awareness of nothingness. When one becomes totally aware of nothingness (non-being), becomes overwhelmed by doubt of existence, logic fades into the nothingness that has overwhelmed a sense of being. Inasmuch as one still has mind, one uses the logic: "If you are aware that you are nothing, you still *are* someone having that awareness." But the very awareness of nothingness soon produces the blown mind. Consciousness of nothingness becomes an eternal insanity which speaks to the human spirit in that totally negative non-existence—thus giving a kind of negative personality to the Devil, the demonic, Satan. This negativeness in no way

4

connotes a weakness. Quite the contrary, there is power to destroy completely human life on earth (there is no destruction in hell, in total non-being: there lurks the empty remains, the nothingness, including pride which ultimately destroys itself in its process of destroying humans on earth).

"For mid the living, I endured it not": among the living on earth, we do not fully endure pride. We put it on! And, because we do, we have the humorous. Without that ever-present tragic dimension of pride on earth, there would be little humor as we know it. (The exception is the finite laughter of the innocent babe.)

> While they rejoice on high, their brightness grows,
> A laughter comes on earth; but down in hell
> A shade grows darker as the spirit saddens.[7]

In earthly existence, pride acts itself out within the total human context, and may be seen through humor as Truth exposes it.

B. *In Humor There Is Truth*

There can be no humor without truth. Whether in finitude or sin-in-finitude, it is truth which is breaking into situations on earth through humor, occasioned by incongruities in human life.

> Schopenhauer suggests that "the cause of laughter in every case is simply the sudden perception of the incongruity between a concept and the real objects" which that concept is supposed to represent . . . humor arises when one suddenly perceives an incongruity between the concept and the object, as in Shakespeare's remark, "There was never yet a philosopher that could endure the toothache patiently."[8]

We have seen the non-being of pride. Truth, as a divine dispensation revealing the being of God, which we all call Being-itself, shows up pride for what it *is-not*. God conquers pride when we know the truth.

1. *When we know the truth about something, this does not mean that we know the mysterious nature of God.* (He could not be a mystery if we could in any manner *ever* know his nature). When we say God is Being-itself, we are not defining God's nature. God is mystery. Any "mystery" understood is not mystery. Comprehending Being-itself remains off bounds for human beings. It is contradictory to think that a human being, as a being created by Being-itself, has the power to grasp the Being-itself which gives it its being. Defining Being-itself would be impossible since Being-itself by its own power gives credibility to what we might say or think about anything, including Being-itself.

> The sacred, then, is the area of mystery. Not mystery in the corrupted sense of an awkward puzzle, nor in the diminished sense of what yet awaits successful investigation. But mystery in the sense of a presence in man's experience of a darkness he knows to be a light that he cannot see, of an intelligibility too bright for his gaze, of a transcendence that evokes his adoration. Mystery is the presence of God. Man cannot with truth locate that presence.[9]

God is not a finite reality, nor could He ever be. What He is in Himself does not and never will come within human knowledge. But He does not choose to remain altogether inaccessible. He has communicated Himself in a kind of knowledge that lies totally outside the grasp of secular disciplines. That knowledge "is equally inaccessible to theology as well. It is an intellectual agnosticism, a sensitivity to what can be known and what will never be knowable. It could be described as the awareness of a total ignorance."[10]

2. *This divine truth, what is and what ought to be, is imaged in our own being.* "This structural centeredness gives man his greatness, dignity, and being, the 'image of God.' It indicates his ability to transcend both himself and his world, to look at both, and to see himself in perspective as the center in which all parts of his world converge."[11] Man was created to be a human being by Being-itself. Human beings refer to

this image of God every time they use the verb *to be.* This does not mean that each is that image of God; but each has the potential of being in that image. Finite human being is the created self made in the image of God. However, even while referring to the *imago dei,* humans actually show a distortion of it.

For example, our "freedom" is not freedom as such, but finite freedom.[12] It starts and continues as an outward quest. Rather than a power causing one to choose, it must be stretched out *for*—and forever eludes. "Man has used his freedom to waste his freedom."[13] We long for infinite freedom, which belongs to God. Being-itself does not stretch out in quest. Being always is; Being-itself is freedom.

Neither is our thinking ability in the image of God. Our cognitive structure is a givenness with which we can relate to ourselves, others, world, and the Creator-Sustainer. It is when we try to relate to the depth of God's Being in ideas that we fail. Paul's reference to wording his prayer points to this dilemma:

> The Spirit too comes to help us in our weakness. For when we cannot choose words in order to pray properly, the Spirit himself expresses our plea in a way that could never be put into words, and God who knows everything in our hearts knows perfectly well what we mean.[14]

Man's emotions express his finitude. They are expressions that man uses to relate to himself, others, his world, and God. Like his thinking (including his thinking that he has freedom), his emotions are learned as he very early begins to kick his way into this world. It is understandable that, when man goes before God in prayer, he goes thinking and he goes *emotionally.* But these states of expressions are the ways we react to this world . . . to God's creation. God sees through the ambiguity of the emotions and the rationality and goes right to the ontic core—man's being—his "I-ness." That set-over-against-us oughtness comes from Being-itself. Man's thinking may be perverted thinking. But it will not be perverted imag-

7

ery of the mind of God. This should not be so difficult to accept since what we think is "out there" in this world is not "out there" at all. What we see "out there" remains merely an idea in our own cognitive structure.[15]

3. Where is truth, then, when a world of varied cultures, societies, governments, religions, and educations are all talking about what is and what is not? Even those within the Christian community differ as to what ought and ought not be. First let it be established that *truth*, what is, *establishes itself from the fact that a negative pre-supposes a positive*. Truth is what is transcending the ambiguity of a good (what is)/evil (what is not) situation. We talk about *what is* all the time and never realize it. Quite unconsciously on our part, all our speech, either explicitly through the voices, moods, tenses, persons, and numbers of the verb *to be* or implicitly through the voices, moods, tenses, persons, and numbers of verbs (i.e. see, saw, will see, shall see, have seen, shall have seen, will have seen, seeing, having seen) point to *what is*, even though the words are a distortion of *what is* since we are estranged from the essential nature of things.

> Every being participates in the structure, but man alone is immediately aware of the structure. It belongs to the character of existence that man is estranged from nature. . . . He can describe the behavior of all things, but he does not know directly what their tragic behavior means to them.[16]

Even when our expressions are distortions, they do express *what is* to us. Being or state of being is explicit in an exclamation: "How beautiful a sunset *is!*" We signal God's presence in life every time we use or imply the verb *to be*.

About non-being we may say, "There is no such thing." We affirm Being-itself in that very statement! This positive nature of Being-itself reveals that even a lie is an expression of truth. For instance, the declaration, "It is a lie" implies: "The truth *is*: it is a lie." Any version of the universal doubter illustrates this positive nature of the spoken word: The father

8

says to his son, "Never say you are certain about anything. You could be wrong." "Are you sure of that, father?" "Yes, I am certain of it."

The more conscious we are in using "to be" or "*not* to be," the more conscious we are of Being-itself and non-being. To illustrate: "I am very happy"—"I am very unhappy." Herein lies the incongruity of the sad clown's humor. He looks sad as he claps his hands, gestures affection for another, laughs, etc. The incongruity in how he looks (how he *is*) over against what he does comes across as laughable. Conversely, the clown with the drastic smile acts sad. The clown may not take himself seriously, but he does take truth seriously—the truth of his own incongruity.

The problem arises concerning what is the absolute truth. It is at this point that Christ comes to the believer as the personification of who we *ought to be*.

> Soul and body must live together with a measure of domestic peace, if wisdom is to be the child of their union, and Christ, like Aristotle, never forgot that this transcendental divorce is wrong no matter which party sues for it. Aristotle converted this insight into a system of metaphysics, while Jesus taught the philosophy inherent in laughter.[17]

4. *Being-itself establishes through the New Being in Christ ("I am who I am"—"I am truth") a unique oughtness within the human situation.* Jesus as truth was the divine-human manifestation of who we ought to be within finitude. "The Fourth Gospel says of him that he *is* truth, but this does not mean that he *has* omniscience or absolute certainty. He *is* the truth in so far as his being—the New Being in him—conquers the untruth of existential estrangement."[18] Oughtness as truth stands beyond where we are and calls us *to be*. Truth as oughtness keeps history going, even when history goes against God. History could not "go against" if there were not that ought-to-beness against which to go. Thus, humanity's biggest wrongs imply a rightness, an oughtness. In that sense God's truth stands as an umbrella of judgment and redemption over

9

our estranged, finite existence. When we become what we ought, we become the being God wants us to be. We break the estrangement and come from our old not-being into our becoming new being.

5. *In experience of truth the New Being in Christ conquers the untruth of prideful actions within existential estrangement.* The exposed non-being of pride is seen for what it is not. Being remains the agent that exposes non-being; that truth becomes for us a New Being. "Being the truth is not the same as knowing the truth about all finite objects and situations."[19] Being truth is not knowing finite space/time facts. Facts alone make us factious—divisive. Finite creatures can be truthful and miss the facts; they can know the facts and be untruthful. One can feed facts into a computer, but one cannot feed into it truth because truth comes in human relationships. Christ is truth in all relationships. His spirit reveals to estranged humanity what humanness is like, who one ought to be, and helps people come to be themselves.

Our relationship with God, then, is not one of knowing His nature, but of knowing Him in faith. We face life when we accept what is revealed through Christ and who we ought to be in this moment through the Holy Spirit. *What is* and *ought to be* was incarnate in Christ ("The divine Spirit was present in Jesus as the Christ without distortion");[20] and possibly accounts for his comment recorded in Luke 12:51, "Do you think that I have come to give you peace on earth? No, I tell you, but rather division." Could "division" here mean "tension"—a feel of the pull of polarities? When what *ought to be* comes into a situation, tension results, and truth works within that tension. When what *ought to be* comes into a family, there can arise conflict within each child and within each parent. When what ought to be comes into life situations, there can be tension, conflict, division. This tension takes place in the process of salvation. Salvation by God begins with a keen awareness of our separation from God—from the *imago dei* whom we ought to be. Part of the tension begins with the realization that, while on the one hand we are aware of separation from God, on the other hand we

10

feel fairly godly as it is. As salvation brings awareness of our ungodliness, there is a "voice" which says that we have taken care of ourselves pretty well thus far. As salvation brings awareness that God's grace bridges the gap, there is something in us that wants to take the credit. We make it seem as if it were an honor for God to reconcile Himself to us. But it is when we know our own sinfulness in our estrangement that we express our dependency upon God. Tension, then, comes within the Christian experience.

Throughout, there is creative tension which causes a new self to be born. We know we are being a new self because the old self remains a real threat. Where there is no conflict, there is no growth. We feel the inner conflict when who we ought to be works on who we are. This tension was working on Jeremiah when he said, "The word of the Lord has become for me a reproach and derision all day long. If I say, I will not mention him or speak any more in his name, there is in my heart as it were a burning fire shut up in my bones, and I am weary with holding it in, and I cannot."[21] When what ought to be comes upon us, it bothers us.

Even after God works the miracle of salvation, one is not saved from tension. The old nature lurks in the shadows of our lives. After Paul's saving experience he said, "I do not understand my own actions. I do not do what I want, but I do the very thing I hate—wretched man that I am. Who will deliver me?" This is genuine human self-transcendence. Standing over against himself Paul saw his wretchedness. It was when he saw God standing over against him that Paul said, "But thanks be to God!"[22]

The infinite blendings of these tensions point to the essential being of finite man. He is of divine potential on the one hand, yet "not there" on the other: his being and non-being that make up his tensions account for his self-creation. Within these tensions man is also beyond his tensions.

6. *Truth, what is and what ought, belongs to God and comes to us from Him who is Being-itself within the total conspectus of all possibilities and non-possibilities, order and disorder, sin and salvation, destruction and construction.*

Being-itself knows what is and what ought, the truth, about the whole makeup of existence from beginning to end. Grace is Being-itself giving unmerited being to human beings. No one earns the right to say, "I am alive." Grace gives a sense of is-ness to this existence. For an alienated person who feels like a nobody, the gift of being somebody is grace.

Truth is a givenness from God, a touch of God in the human situation. Truth is a spirit that transcends every human expression of truth. Thus, the statement, "it is the truth," remains a spirit, a dimension, beyond our words about the truth. Truth may turn the self in a direction other than what the facts seem to indicate. What to us seem to be the facts may be crystallized into logical propositions and not be the truth at all. Truth may come through parable, paradox, analogy, example, etc., but will never be contained in any of these figures of speech. Or it may be "told" through silence.

The selfhood which has been distorted out of shape through the non-being of pride is constantly being called back to the whole being through what is and ought to be. "The essential nature of man is present in all stages of his development, although in existential distortion."[23] We intensify estrangement from our true self through intentional ignorance concerning our real motives. "One of the most striking facts about the dynamics of human personality is the intentional ignorance concerning one's real motives."[24] This mixture of non-being through pride estranges us from our true self and accounts for the ambiguities with our multi-dimensional unity (cultural, religious, moral, theological, sociological, etc.). When truth, what humans ought to be, strikes what a person *thinks* he/she is (in pride), humor results.

Charlie Chaplin said that he made people laugh by telling them the plain truth of things. Will Rogers acknowledged that he would not be very humorous if it were not for the government. He did not make jokes. He just watched the government and reported the facts! Max Eastman says:

> Our lives in all departments consist so largely of the cultivation of insubstantial pretenses and amenities, the

feeding of think glamours—or posturing and pretending, sometimes honorable, sometimes with self-contempt— that almost any perfectly candid speech about anything contains an element of release. . . . It is not truth as such, of course, that is a joke. The joke is to have some other trend of expectation, one perhaps belonging to our cultural or stucco selves, so playfully to smash, and in the wreckage find this deeper satisfaction to our sense of what is real. The face of truth is a strange face, at which when it obtrudes suddenly we cannot help but smile, and yet it is also an intimately familiar face, and notwithstanding our perpetual flight from it, well loved. That is why it falls so nearly in with the operation of a joke. It disappoints a superficial expectation but satisfies an underlying trend.[25]

Humor comes off, not by a display of how funny we think we are, but by a commitment to truth: "Truth is so necessary a property of a jest, that we may affirm a false jest is no jest at all. Truth is the fundamental perfection of all our knowledge, which falls away at once, if without the support of truth."[26]

C. *Truth Reveals Itself by Eliciting Incongruities*

1. *Ontic incongruities trigger finite humor.* Our finitude is derived from our creation to be out of nothing (*ex nihilo*),[27] consequently ruling non-being out of the essential nature of things. But non-being is still there as a negative participant with our essential nature in finitude. And it plays a major role in humor, putting human beings into playful humor. A baby may keep a straight face while a bottle of orange juice is before him. When it is suddenly taken away, the surprise of not-there-ness triggers the laugh.

2. *But sin-in-finitude perverts these ontic incongruities.* When the will comes into play, ontic incongruities that make the child laugh lose their appeal to make the adult laugh. We call adult humor "mature" (sarcasm intended), when in fact we become so swamped with pretensions and self-deceptions

that our humor loses its naturalness. That loss results in immaturity. A child's natural humor is mature; an adult's unnatural humor is immature. Sin-in-finitude causes a change of form within the ontic incongruities (here it is; there it is not). Sin mixes things up. What we say is there may not be there; or it may be there but how we say it is there is not there. It may not be there when we say it is not there, but it ought to be! But we can still laugh at incongruities, perverted or not.

3. *Humor within sin-caused ambiguous incongruities comes off redemptively when we laugh at our efforts to determine what is and what is not. Our actions are ludicrous when we who are made out of nothing try to make something out of nothing, when we try to act like the Creator.*

The act becomes funnier the better we understand that area of divine activity: God creates us out of nothing and uses non-being in actualizing our potential, in helping us be somebody.

> Being, limited by non-being, is finitude. Non-being appears as the "not yet" of being and as the "no more" of being. It confronts that which is with a definite end (*finis*). This is true of everything except Being-itself—which is not a "thing." As the power of being, Being-itself cannot have a beginning and an end. Otherwise it would have arisen out of non-being. But non-being is literally nothing except in relation to being. Being precedes non-being in ontological validity, as the word "non-being" itself indicates. Being is the beginning without a beginning, the end without an end. It is its own beginning and end, the initial power of everything that is. However, everything which participates in the power of being is mixed with non-being. It is being in the process of becoming from and going toward non-being. It is finite.[28]

That out-of-nothing aspect of human existence threatens existence at every turn and can only be managed through one's courage to be out and going. Non-being cannot be called good or bad since it lacks quality. But it can be awe-fully bad (tragic) for one when one is not a human *being*. On the other hand, it can be very good for one who has the courage to be in spite of non-being. As one has that God-given courage to be in spite of non-being, it can be said that non-being as *ouk on* (absolute negation of being) participates in our potential being. The more threats one meets in courage (and they do not come easier with practice), the stronger one becomes. The power of courage is not one's own. The task is not simply to work up a sweat but to participate in a power to be that is not grounded in one's own innate capabilities. The strength gained in this exercise does not make non-being virtuous; it means Being-itself is all-powerful in the redemptive handling of non-being for our sake. With this meager understanding of God's control and use of non-being (though non-being is everything except "Godly"), the more ludicrous becomes the creature-man who talks with God as if he were a co-equal.

4. When we think we can handle non-being ourselves, when we try to do that which only God can do, we look ludicrous. This brings us to the thrust of non-being in its tragic dimension. *The tragic aspect of non-being comes from sin-in-finitude, as we pridefully interpret finiteness as infiniteness.* Obviously one is not being oneself in acting this way. When one sees the tragic aspect of non-being, one can see a person acting like what he is not—and laugh.

In this laughter, one may experience self-transcendence. He has been fooled by something, and now he recognizes it. While being in playful humor, one waits to be fooled again and again. Each laugh can signal another experience of self-transcendence. This humor-triggered self-transcendence begins in finitude (as seen in the laughter of a baby) and continues within sin-in-finitude (as seen in laughter within tragedy). Whether in finitude or in sin-in-finitude, laughter in itself signals that self-transcendence may be taking place.

We have glanced at humor in the innocence of finitude. Now we look at humor in sin-in-finitude seen in relationship to tragedy. "It is impossible to speak meaningfully to tragedy without understanding the ambiguity of greatness. . . . The

15

tragic can be understood only on the basis of the understanding of greatness." [29] A baby reveals itself in the ontic process of laughter (being playful). That same finite greatness expressed in self-transcendence via laughter goes throughout human existence and gets tangled with tragedy when man identifies "himself with that to which self-transcendence is directed—the great itself. He does not resist self-transcendence, but he resists the demand to transcend his own greatness."[30] At this point, when human beings fix upon their own greatness and refuse to accept their limitations as absolutes, the tragic results. Humanity's greatness ambiguously united with *hubris*, "the self-elevation of the great beyond the limits of its finitude,"[31] accounts for destruction of self and others. This extension of oneself beyond finiteness results in a manifestation of non-being—the tragic.

Being in playful humor can redeem the greatness/tragedy ambiguity by energizing again the process of self-transcendence, humanity's true greatness. Self-transcendence expressed in being in good humor removes one far enough from the tragic to laugh at it. Many of the subjects of adult humor are distinctly unfunny. "What are most jokes about, and what have they been about through the ages? Mothers-in-law, unpaid bills, drunks, taxes, tramps, corpses, excretory functions, politicians, vermin, bad taste, bad breaks, sexual ineptitudes, pomp, egotism, stinginess and stupidity." [32] As unpleasant as these subjects can be, there is in every one of them an element which, if we were playful, could become funny. Yet, the closer we get to the subject of the humor, the less we feel like being playful. We are not true to the ontology of humor when we make the claim that something innately is or is not funny. About the same thing one may claim, "It is funny," and another may say, "It is serious." And both are being true to their experience with it. Each person's comment expresses his/her own distance from it. A warning flag goes up at this point; some subjects are too serious to laugh at, namely, God, love, faith, etc. These experiences lie within the framework of Truth-itself. Ontologically, Truth

16

cannot be laughed at since Truth is the congruous quality that elicits incongruities. W. C. Fields said it this way:

> I never saw anything funny that wasn't terrible. If it causes pain, it's funny; if it doesn't, it isn't. I try to pretend that it isn't painful. I try to hide the pain with embarrassment, and the more I do that, the better they like it. But that doesn't mean they are unsympathetic. Oh, no, they laugh often with tears in their eyes. Only of course it mustn't be *too* painful. I never would try to make love funny, for instance. I was in love once myself, and that's too painful—that's too painful![33]

When the human being in play interacts with life's unpleasant happenings and turns them around, the more firmly the potential redemption of the tragic is established.

By self-transcendence we can be removed far enough from these areas to laugh. The humor is not directed at the person in tragedy (though on the surface that looks like the case). It is directed at the tragic aspect of their lives, at *hubris* gone wild, at non-being. Jesus Christ loved people; yet He ridiculed their *hubris*: "You have such a fine way of rejecting the commandments of God."[34] He pointed out their "fine" way in a ludicrous statement: "You strain at a gnat and swallow a camel."[35] Those toward whom these remarks were directed accepted the tragic as a way of life. They had the power (which proved to be their failure). While participating with this greatness/tragedy ambiguity in their lives Jesus used humor freely, thus permitting in his own humanity the greatness to prevail over the potentially tragic. His own self-transcendence continued throughout his involvement with human tragedy, and humor was a part of it.

Jesus expressed no humor-at-self on the cross because there was no *hubris*-gone-wild in his life to make for any self-humor. Jesus overcame the tragic dimension of human existence (always a potential in his life) in his death by entrusting his life to God: "Father, into thy hands I commend my Spirit." *Hubris* rebels against death or destroys one's self, and this is not the spirit of Christ.

17

But the humorous surrounds the cross. We can see the tragedy that surrounds the cross in the lives of those who had the power. They hung Christ on the cross to restore peace and order! They put Him out of the way because He was not religious! Not good enough! They had a "fine" way of rejecting the commandments of God. Tragic man many laugh at Christ off or on the cross. But the last laugh is on the one who tries it. They tried it by putting on him the crown of thorns, the purple robe, and the mocking title "King of the Jews" on a sign over his head. And they laughed at him. But their mockery backfired when their projected order was smashed by those who used their same reasoning: the Jews had to be conquered to maintain peace and order. Then Romans ruled the world ruthlessly in maintaining *their* definition of peace and order. And then the Roman-protected order was smashed by those who used the same reasoning: *that* order had to be conquered to maintain peace and order. Truly, the human tragedy becomes compounded. And so do the ironies of human actions; we miss our greatness when we act great and powerful! It is to our credit—a sign of our self-transcendence, our finite greatness—when we laugh with Christ at the tragic in ourselves and others who throughout time stand around the cross of Christ.

Alienation from one's true self accounts for existential anxiety, that inner tension between one's becoming and not becoming oneself. As we try to become on our own, to be the God of our own life, it turns out that our *not becoming* pushes to the forefront, thus revealing the tragedy of our existence. Kierkegaard saw that both "the tragic and the comic are the same, insofar as both are based on contradiction." [36] While the tragic apprehension of the contradiction despairs of a way out, the comic interpretation cancels the contradiction and renders it less painful. This does not mean that the tragic apprehension is "bad." Tragic insight recognizes the good/evil ambiguities within the contradiction; the humorous reaction resolves the contradiction without destroying the tragic insight. Because of this relatedness, humor may come in the worst forms of human sufferings.

5. The inner reaction to this becoming/not-becoming tension inevitably spills over in expressions of laughter and tears.

> Humor finds its basis in the congruity of life itself, the contrast between the fretting cares and the petty sorrows of the day and the long mystery of the tomorrow. Here laughter and tears become one, and the humor becomes the contemplation and interpretation of our life.[37]

Laughter and tears are the two faces we use in expressing the moment's reaction to tragedy. In the same tragic context it is easy to turn from laughter to tears and from tears to laughter within split seconds. We even laugh through our tears, cry through our laughter. To discover the funny in the tragic human situation, one does not squelch tears. In a stone-faced countenance, this would hold back the possibility of the humorous coming through. To help us discover the ludicrous in tragic circumstances, God's truth spotlights the worthwhile, the meaningful, what is. That meaningful remembrance might be a glimpse of an incongruity. And in that glimpse with truth of the incongruity one laughs. God redeems the tragic through tears and laughter.

To illustrate: Once I received word that one of my parishioners, a lady whose body had been invaded by cancer, wanted to see me. Obviously, I knew I had to talk to her about her physical state. But when I got there, she said very confidently, "I can live with my cancer; it is my husband who is about to kill me. Just about the time I get to sleep in the early morning hours, he wakes me up to see if I am dead!" We both had to laugh at that statement, but it was true. Her biggest problem was not cancer but her husband. He had gone to a "prophetess," who had foretold when his wife would die. To his sick wife it seemed as if her husband were helping to prove the seer right! The thing that I remember about that conversation was that, as she was telling it in tears, she began to laugh at how beautifully humorous it all seemed to be. Her problem with her husband was as real to her as her battle with cancer. I can still hear her say:

19

"I know he loves me and is concerned for me, but he is about to kill me in showing it!"

Another illustration points to this laughter/tears relationship: For the last half dozen or so years of his life, Ed was the life of the party whenever the Senior Citizens gathered for their recreation. In his Brooklyn accent he would attempt to sing Irish songs, and he would put on a pretty good show. After Ed died, I was called to the home where I met with his widow whom we all called Burt, and with Shirley, their only daughter. Until this time Shirley had reacted with stoic self-composure. But when Burt asked me if I had heard about the day that Shirley got married and then continued to tell me about the occasion, Shirley broke into tears and laughter. Her reaction was understandable as the story was told. On that wedding day, when he stood at the altar of the church, the minister asked, "Who giveth this woman to be married to this man?" and there was no answer. Again the minister asked, "Who giveth this woman to be married to this man?" and there was no answer. A third time this happened, and no answer. Finally Ed in his short frame stood up straight and said, "I won't give her away. She is mine, and will be mine as long as I live. I will lend her to you, but I will not give her away!" and he sat down.

On the day of the funeral service, I reminded the congregation of the particular little act by which Ed usually could be identified. Eighty-year-old Ed had a way of coming into a room of people and purposely tripping himself, as if he were going to fall. People were always reaching to catch the little man, but he never fell. As I recall the story to the bereaved that day, again I can see smiles and tears.

It should be noted in these illustrations that humor, as a contemplation of life, excludes utter giddiness or superciliousness. "Since the ludicrous involves perception of an absurdity, it excludes foolishness, pure silliness, senselessness. The ludicrous encounter must yield not blindness but an insight."[38]

6. *Humor*, in pointing beyond the veil of laughter and tears, *participates redemptively in divine providence*. Within

20

tragic human circumstances direction is coming through humor.

> Providence is "the divine condition" which is present in every group of finite conditions and in the totality of finite conditions. It is not an additional factor, a miraculous physical or mental interference in terms of supernaturalism. It is the quality of inner-directedness present in every situation. The man who believes in providence does not believe that a special divine activity will alter the condition of finitude and estrangement. He believes, and asserts with the courage of faith, that no situation whatsoever can frustrate the fulfillment of his ultimate destiny, that nothing can separate him from the love of God which is in Christ Jesus. (Romans 8).[39]

Humor triggers the glimpse of the gap between the estranged sinful self (what is) and the essential self, the *imago dei* (what ought to be). "What ought to be and what is are identical in the state of potentiality. In existence this identity is broken, and in every life process the identity and non-identity of what is and what ought to be are mixed." [40] The incongruity between who we are and who we ought to be can be glimpsed through humor. Any time one says about another, "He has such a good sense of humor," one is saying, "He has a quick sense of man's incongruities."

Since the non-being of pride (who we think we are) plays a part in humor, there always remains that tragic aspect of humor. Pride boasts our self-importance while truth reveals what we are really like. The incongruity may ripple into wit, wrinkle into irony, or erupt in laughter (or tears). Whichever the case, pride is revealed for what it really is, and the *imago dei* is revealed for what human nature essentially is; making humor potentially redemptive in pointing one to one's true self. Insofar as humor does help one rise above the tragic, humor participates in this genuine paradox in the form of redemption. When one sees the humor, one conquers the tragic. One lives meaningfully with the tragic.

For instance, one can say, "He is timid," and get a laugh

if the person to whom one refers acts anything but timid! The emphasis here is on *acts like*. An element of tragedy revolves around the negative fact that some people *are* timid (a particular expression of universal human insecurity); to that extent they are non-being themselves. But we can laugh at that tragic aspect when a timid person acts like he is not timid (comic actors again and again witness to their temerity). This turns out to be an ironic twist of humor: we call an extrovert timid and laugh, when he may very well be; and that is tragic. But that remains a function of humor: it redeems the tragic aspect of human existence. A Christian sociologist puts it this way:

> Finally (and this is the most important in the last resort), the Christian faith looks at human existence and human society under the aspect of redemption. This means that it can afford to take the world less seriously than it takes itself. Christian debunking is therefore free from . . . bitterness and humorlessness.[41]

a. Bad humor comes when the person referred to as "timid" acts that way, when non-being cowers him into hopelessness. *Bad humor comes when incongruities are imagined wholly within the frame of non-being.* Such fantasy incongruities are untruthful, therefore non-essential, no matter how "positive" sounding one spells out the gap of a situation. There is no gap without truth to elicit it. To illustrate: Nazis experienced sick laughter as they fed humans to the ovens. They imagined the Jews were inferior to how the Jews acted, *no matter how they acted*. There was no good act because there was no good Jew. That viewpoint provided the basis for an imagined glimpse of the incongruity whenever they saw a learned Jew suffering. They thought it was funny. When incongruities are fantasized with non-being, it is bad humor, because there are no incongruities in non-being. Ontologically speaking, then, bad humor finally is not humor at all. "As is often said, the comic involves an affirmation of life—perhaps instead of being really funny, the so-called

22

'comedies' of the genre of *Arsenic and Old Lace*, of childhood murderers, besotted drunkards, and mechanical supermen, are rather signs of aesthetic confusion." [42]

b. Within that same social setting of human suffering and bad humor, there was as well good humor, the only kind of true humor there is. We refer here to Viktor Frankl who had lost his wife and children to the ovens. He was starved and naked, yet he said:

> Humor was another of the soul's weapons in the fight for self-preservation. It is well known that humor, more than anything else in the human makeup, can afford an aloofness and an ability to rise above any situation, even if only for a few seconds. I practically trained a friend of mine who worked next to me on the building site to develop a sense of humor. I suggested to him that we would promise each other to invent at least one amusing story daily, about some incident that could happen one day after our liberation. He was a surgeon and had been an assistant on the staff of a large hospital. So I once tried to get him to smile by describing to him how he would be unable to lose the habits of camp life when he returned to his former work. On the building site (especially when the supervisor made his tour of inspection) the foreman encouraged us to work faster by shouting: "Action! Action!" I told my friend, "One day you will be back in the operating room, performing a big abdominal operation. Suddenly an orderly will rush in announcing the arrival of the senior surgeon by shouting, 'Action! Action!'" [43]

For Viktor Frankl, humor was a Godsend. His situation dramatically illustrates the redemptive quality of laughter. It kept him from being pushed into non-being. Indeed, it remained the laugh at himself (and non-being within the self-incongruity) that defeated non-being, that even used non-being to assert his own self-hood. Humor permitted him to live within tragedy without letting it get him down. A dead serious person in that situation of human folly, sin, and igno-

23

rance would have been a dead person. Frankl did not laugh at what was happening. But he did laugh at himself taking his finite experiences as if they had eternal importance. That self-transcending experience through humor brought out the greatness of the prisoners, a greatness the Nazis never saw and the ingredient their humor never knew.

c. Humor redemptively carried one man, with all his ponderous ontology, through the last hours of his life. *The tension in Paul Tillich's dying day was relieved by jest.* In Rollo May's biography we read of Tillich's last day on earth:

> When the doctor came in about noon, Paulus joked with him. "Today I'm going to be a complete ascetic. I spent a long time yesterday figuring out the menu for today, but I'm not going to eat a thing." The doctor laughed outright. "That's the first time I ever heard it put that way." [44]

d. When we see what God sees in us, then we may see our incongruities, and thus the humor. When we see, with God, our incongruities, it is good humor; without God's insight into our situation, it is bad humor. Humor then can be a matter of life or death. Both of these states of being and non-being are experienced in human relationships in the here and now. This ambiguity of what is and what is not lies within the being/non-being of humans, not in the being of God, Being-itself. God in His mind sees incongruities in us and shares His insight with us by spotlighting with truth those incongruities. We can laugh because God does.

Some create their own incongruities by identifying themselves with God on the throne in heaven laughing. Those who think they have captured the laugh of God can only laugh at others, not at themselves. When one under truth sees this laugh of God, one may then laugh with God at oneself. A self-transcending laugh of fulfillment comes as we laugh with God at our "laugh of God."

When an estranged person elevates himself to the level of what he thinks is his potential greatness, he leads himself down the tragic road of self-destruction. When that person sees under truth what he is doing to himself, nursing his own greatness, beauty, intellect, power, he sees the ludicrous. A laugh at one's self can lead to one's acceptance of finitude, weakness, errors, ignorance, insecurity, and anxiety. When one through humor recognizes his *hubris*, in that moment of self-transcendence he affirms self-hood within existential estrangement and reveals his true greatness, his *hubris* in humility.

There is nothing laughable about our relationship with God. We are laughable when we see our real selves in relation to our false selves under the surveillance of God's truth, when we see that what we thought was actual about ourselves is actually false. When we realize under God's truth that we are *false*, we are becoming in the re-creative sense ourselves. We then seriously thank God that we can laugh at our ludicrous selves. Without this redemptive aspect of humor, we would have to agree with the metaphysical conclusion of Leacock: "All ends with a cancellation of forces and comes to nothing; and our universe ends thus with one vast, silent, unappreciated joke."[45] With the redemptive aspect of humor, life's metaphysical incongruities are resolved into an enveloping harmony, into a sense of well-being. This latter resolve comes through the leap of faith which says that God accepts us in our world of comic errors and sin, which says that Being-itself affirms our being as we trust that He knows better for us than we know for ourselves.

D. *The Human Being in Playful Humor Reacts to Ontic Incongruities*

1. We have seen how truth elicits the gaps of incongruity that triggers humor, which in turn reveals the truth. The fact that we have used pondersome ontological categories to dig into the makeup of humor itself smacks of incongruity if we assume that such stark seriousness has answered the humor question. That would be a laugh. In order for our musings to reveal truth we must stay close to experiential truth, which

brings us back to the two basic ways that incongruities in finitude and sin-in-finitude trigger humor in the human being in play. Max Eastman did not analyze jokes to arrive at a definition. He observed the two ways that people laugh in the laughter of a good-natured baby.

> I am convinced that the majority of the learned philosophers who have written treatises on laughter and the comic never saw a baby. And by seeing a baby I mean having an opportunity to look one over calmly and deliberately and without being afraid that somebody is going to ask you to hold it.
>
> The next time you are called upon to entertain a baby, I will tell you what to do. Laugh, and then make a perfectly terrible face. If the baby is old enough to perceive faces, and properly equipped for the calamities of the life that lies before him, he will laugh too. But if you make a perfectly terrible face all of a sudden without laughing, he is more likely to scream with fright. In order to laugh at a frightful thing he has to be in a mood of play.
>
> If that perceptual effort is beyond him, try a practical joke. Offer him something that he wants a little and will reach out to get, and when he is about to grasp it, jerk it *smilingly away*. Again he may set up a yell of indignation, or he may emit a rollicking and extreme cackle, a kind of kicking scream, as though at the most ingenious joke ever perpetrated since Adam lost a rib.
>
> Those are the two orthodox ways of entertaining a baby. And they correspond to two of the most famous definitions of the comic ever given. Aristotle defined the comic as "some defect or ugliness which is not painful or destructive," and added: "For example, the comic mask is ugly and distorted but does not cause pain." In other words, it is *making terrible faces playfully*.
>
> . . . Another famous philosopher, Immanuel Kant, defined the cause of laughter as "The sudden transformation of a strained expectation into nothing"—or in other words, *as reaching after something and finding that it is not there*.[46]

The first burst of humor discussed by Max Eastman comes

when the baby sees the incongruity between the two faces in a playful spirit. The second burst of humor comes when the "rug is jerked from under the baby," so to speak, when what was expected to follow suddenly is gone, and what is left gives humorous satisfaction. In the former case the baby was amused and humor resulted; in the latter the baby was teased and humor resulted. The former looked funny; the latter incongruity (now it is; and now it is not) brought surprise and humorous reaction. Let us refer to these two reactions as funny-looking humor (ludicrous) and rug-pulling humor (witty). There remains this difference between conveying ludicrous impressions and cracking practical jokes:

> Practical jokes, for instance, have to start off *plausibly* and collapse *suddenly*. A ludicrous impression can be preposterous right from the start, if the comedian has your interested attention; and suddenness, though it may add a charm, is wholly unessential to it. "Neatness," so almost absolute a law for practical jokes, would be the strangulation of poetic humor. And "timing," although it has value in all arts, is not the crucial thing in painting funny pictures that it is in making witty cracks.[47]

2. Incongruities elicited by the witty and the ludicrous will remain unseen if one *is not* in playful humor. Like the wind the humor will breeze past; unlike the wind, one will not feel a thing. Now comes the question for the student of humor: how does one write down the witty and the ludicrous revealed by incongruities? At this juncture we can go to the figures of speech that have arisen through the years in the English language quite spontaneously to express the ontology of varied situations. Man expressed how things *were* (remember *to be* points to finite conditions even in perversion); grammarians put it down and analyzed the mechanics within the ontic expression. Out of this exercise came the figures of speech. *Inherent in each figure of speech is an ontology and a vehicle for expressing ontological incongruities*. We will now look at those figures of speech and illustrate how they can be used as a vehicle for the witty and the ludicrous. Hope-

fully this exercise will be looked upon as illustrative of the ontology of humor rather than mere redundancy of the ontology of humor already laid out.

Incongruities Expressed Through Figures of Speech:

A strategic deviation from ordinary word arrangement produces figures of speech called *schemes*. Those schemes given to ontological incongruity are:

(1) *Antithesis*—scheme of balance: "I taught you everything you know and you still don't know nothing." The double negative, "don't know nothing," furnishes within itself one incongruity, i.e., If you don't know nothing, it means you know something. But this is the opposite of the intent of the sentence. Ontologically there cannot be two negatives in polarity. The juxtaposition of the negative, non-being, has to be positive. The hearer gets a stronger sense of the incongruity that the one spoken to *is not* so smart as he *thinks he is* because of the ontological bungling in the use of the double negative. But this double negative observation is superimposed on the antithesis itself. "I taught you everything you know" is the thesis. The antithesis is, "You still don't know nothing." This word arrangement reveals the speaker's own ontological incongruity, in that who he *thinks he is* (a know-it-all) is not who he *really* is (in his criticism he acts as though he knows all, while at the same time he uses poor grammar.)

(2) *Anastrophe*—scheme of unusual or inverted word order: The man claimed to know all about his wife. *But her size he did not know.* The two sentences taken together constitute an antithesis. The last italicized sentence is an anastrophe.

This scheme can be effective in gaining attention; however, its chief purpose is to secure emphasis. In this example the anastrophe is used for emphasis in a humorous context. The incongruity lies in the husband so secure in his own mind that he knew his wife, when in fact he did not even know what size dress she wore.

(3) *Parenthesis*—scheme of unusual word order: As I stood before the judge, he said to me, "Did you pull your car out of this intersection into the left front fender of this lady's car?" (Yes, a woman driver!) And I said, "Your honor, . . ."

28

This brief insertion interrupts the normal flow of the sentence, and in this example furnishes an incongruity in revealing a male chauvinist driver who had wrecked a woman's car.

(4) *Apposition*—Men with names like Francis, Judy, Jewel, and Dot sometimes have difficult times cashing their checks. In a parenthesis the words are not needed for the sentence to make sense. In an apposition the words are needed in order to have a complete sentence.

The incongruity lies in a female name being given to a male. One may be one thing while his name implies another. In this case the man may be the stereotyped muscle man. That makes the ludicrous obvious to a heterosexually oriented audience. If he overplays his male role to the point of toughness, the ludicrous becomes more obvious as the incongruity becomes more pronounced.

(5) *Ellipsis*—scheme of omission of words obviously understood: I viewed my potential in the mirror, every line, every missing hair, and discovered I had plenty!

In this deliberate omission of words implied by the context the incongruity lies in seeing who we really are over against who we would like to be so much that we try to *make up* the difference.

(6) *Asyndeton*—scheme of omission of conjunctions: I came, I preached, I went home, I got preached to. An Asyndeton can be said to be an ellipsis that has only to do with omission of conjunctions.

In this omission of conjunctions (a technique especially good for conclusions) the incongruity lies in the sudden switch of roles. A preacher being preached to is taken off his pedestal. He *is not* what he (or we) make him out to be.

(7) *Alliteration*—by repetition of the same letter or sounds at the beginning of two or more consecutive words or of words near one another: The professor, stumbled, stuttered, and struggled through his lecture on "The Art of Public Speaking."

(8) *Assonance*—He said he wanted to grow to be real old, get real sick, and then get well.

The ontological incongruity here lies in one not accepting

death as a state of his finite human beingness while he makes himself think that life here on earth is forever.

(9) *Anaphora*—The comic's fame came. His fame lived. His fame died. He labors to resurrect his funniness. He works so hard at it that when people do laugh he wonders why they did (a paradox used with anaphora).

This use of the same words beginning successive clauses sets up the incongruity. Nothing is more ludicrous than one trying to be funny. He is not what he thinks he is.

(10) *Epistrophe*—For two hours he aced his serve. He lobbed the ball. He put a top spin, a back spin, on the ball. He played the angle shots with the ball. Everything went well; and when he got on court, he never saw the ball!

While repetition of the same words at the end of successive clauses is good for emphasis, in this example it plays a role in the setting up of an incongruity. The tennis player is very good in his mind until he gets on court. Then the real player (or *non*-player) comes out. He *is not* what he thinks he is.

(11) *Epanalepsis*—repetition at the end of a clause of the word that occurred at the beginning of the clause. To illustrate: Player chased player. Hard serve followed hard serve. Ace followed ace. And I won—until I got on the court. (The same ontological setting as epistrophe, above.)

(12) *Anadiplosis*— repetition of the last word of one clause at the beginning of the following clause: The Israelites brought their sacrifices and complaints to God. God was not treating *them* right. They complained how God had short-changed them while they brought their crippled, blind, diseased old sheep and moldy bread to sacrifice as a symbol of their fidelity to God. (Anadiplosis in hyperbole.)

(13) *Climax*—arrangement of words, phrases, or clauses in an order of increasing importance:

Climax does not lend itself easily to the use of humor because the climax normally does not point to an incongruity, but to congruity. However, when the last term of a climax refers to an obvious incongruity, humor results. That little drippy-nosed street-corner urchin might one day become a great teacher, a big business tycoon, the president of the

30

United States, or a Methodist preacher. (Making the "Methodist preacher" an equal of the U.S. president creates an image of someone higher in importance than he really is).

(14) *Antimetabole*— repetition of words, in successive clauses, in reverse grammatical order, used to reinforce antithesis: He practiced preaching to the cabbage heads as if they were people. He preached to the people as if they were cabbage heads. (People normally do not see themselves as cabbage heads. However, most of us know that we often act with as much intelligence as a cabbage head).

(15) *Chiasmus*—the ("criss-cross") reversal of grammatical structures in successive phrases or clauses: He discovers dandruff on his neighbor's coat, but with his brush-off of scalp debris too much talent shows. (This self-righteous critic puts himself *above* his counterpart and in his action reveals a manner contradictory to who he thinks he is).

(16) *Polypton*—repetition of words derived from the same root: She chose to be chosen for the festival duchess. And humbly accepted the public's recognition of her place in the parade. (Litotes with polypton.) When one sets up his own setting for recognition, and then receives his favors *humbly*, the incongruity of his actions comes from the sin of pride.

A transference of meaning produces figures of speech called *tropes*. Those tropes given to ontological incongruities are:

(1) *Metaphor*—She is a Christian go-go girl.

(a) *Allegory*—extended metaphor: She is a Christian go-go girl, who shows how to do good at a pace which makes things happen. Her very name means that Christ *has* come. He has come in the teachings she has brought to the ignorant, in the love given to the unloved, in the faith lived in the midst of trouble.

(b) *Parable*—There was a woman who taught the ignorant, loved the unloved, and had faith in the midst of trouble. She fed the poor and visited the sick. Her readiness to act made her a Christian go-go girl. The Kingdom of God is made up of Christian go-go girls.

(c) *Simile*—She is like a Christian go-go-girl.

(2) *Synechdoche*—the part stands for the whole, or the whole for the part: The hustler in the pool hall prays, "Give me this day my daily bread."

(3) *Metonymy*—substitution of some suggestive word for what is actually meant: At the church he drank a *jigger*; at home he drank the *bottle*.

(4) *Pun*—a play on words.

(a) *Antanaclosis*—repetition of a word in two different senses: When we think we excel in intelligence, we may excel in losing friends.

(b) *Paronomasia*—use of words alike in sound but different in meaning: We accept who we are, whether we have a high I.Q. or make a low miscue.

(c) *Syllepsis*—use of a word understood differently in relation to two or more other words, which it modifies or governs: He broadcasts his sermons and his humility.

(d) *Zeugma*—somewhat like syllepsis, but whereas in syllepsis the single word is gramatically and idiomatically compatible with both of the other words, in a zeugma the single word does not fit the other two: The contractor was less interested in concretizing a street than he was his relations with a certain attractive blond.

(5) *Anithimeria*—the substitution of one part of speech for another: *String* your finger and you will remember not to forget.

(6) *Periphrasis*—substitution of a descriptive word or phrase for a proper name or of a proper name for a quality associated with the name: Ever since "Jumping Jehoshaphat" jumped, we have been calling on him to perform for us in times of stress.

(7) *Personification*—investing abstractions or inanimate objects with human qualities or abilities: The tractor coughed, sputtered, and burped as it came to life on a cold morning in January.

(8) *Hyperbole*—the use of exaggerated terms for purpose of emphasis or heightened effect: He was so pious that he broke his date because she wore "My Sin."

(9) *Litotes*—deliberate use of understatement for humor: When the parrot called, "Come in," we did. And found the lady of the house busy. She was nude and grabbing for cover.

(10) *Rhetorical Question*—asking question for purpose of putting forth a plea: How attentive are we really? Some men do not even know the size dress their wives wear. They can tell the size of every deer they killed, but don't know the size of their wives.

(11) *Irony*—conveys meaning opposite to its literal meaning: Our teeth decay while we live and stop decaying when we die. A humorous observation: "My teeth are rotting; that means I am alive and well."

(a) *Sarcasm*—bitter irony with intent to ridicule: Ted Kennedy is such a fine Christian man—and a good swimmer too.

(b) *Cynicism*—to accept mockingly the negative governing factor in human conduct: Man is the only animal that makes a virtue out of his unselfishness. He only wants to make happy the lady with whom he is having an affair.

(c) *Sardonic*—characterized by derision or scorn, skeptically humorous: It will work because, of course, *you* said it would.

(d) *Invective*—insult; abusive diatribe: He is a pointy-headed politician with barely enough sense to keep from walking backwards.

(e) *Satire*—any criticism or censure relying on exposure, often by irony, of the subtle, ridiculous, or absurd qualities of something. It ridicules the conduct, beliefs, or institutions disapproved by the author: At the Charity Ball all the benefits were to go to build an animal shelter for the local Humane Society. Guests included a local road-building contractor who spent the evening trying to sell his sewer plans to a city commissioner, who was more interested in concretizing his relations with a certain attractive blond than he was a street. After the party all agreed that the *benefit* was a great success (Last pun complements satire).

(12) *Whimsy*—a sudden, impulsive change of mind: You

could never convince me to be a bishop—how much does a bishop make?

(13) *Onomatopoeia*—use of words whose sound echoes the the sense: The broken mixer squealed, moaned, and groaned in pain. I sat there and rubbed it, petted it, held its little handle until its squeals and moans ceased.

(14) *Oxymoron*—the yoking of two terms that are ordinarily contradictory: She is a cheerful pessimist who enjoys telling others that they are going to hell.

(15) *Paradox*—(oxymoron's close kin): He believed that he had complete control over his emotions. When his wife cried, he philosophied. When his daughter had an affair with her married college professor, he *understood*. As his bookkeeper embezzled money, he insisted that it was merely a mistake. His wife divorced him; his daughter looked elsewhere for direction; he lost his business. He had peptic ulcers, hypertension, and a spastic colon. But through it all he kept his cool. (Paradox: In finding his "cool," he lost it all).

Writings naturally will contain a mixture or a blending of different parts of speech. The following three allegories illustrate this.

(1) What would we do without the plastic man? (Rhetorical question.) He says, "I'm everything and nothing. I am on the road, but not to anywhere in particular. Send not to ask who I am, because by the time you get through, I will be something else."[48] His nature is borrowed from the social system which needs plastic, a cheap synthetic fabric adaptable to a multitude of purposes without having much of an identity itself.[49] He is that colorful fork (metaphor) you eat with at the picnic. With a little more than a little pressure, he breaks. When the heat is on, he bends, loses his color, and fades away into uselessness (personification). We appreciate the fine qualities of gold and steel. Who wants to cuddle up to a heart of plastic, or march into battle with a leader who has nerves of plastic? (Personification in a rhetorical question.) If you raise your hand to signal "I do," look at the hand. It may be turning to plastic!

(2) Who is the darling? (Rhetorical question.) He knows that he looks adorable. He turns on the holy look every time he passes near a camera. He would not want to deprive the less fortunate of such a fine photogenic subject as himself (sarcasm). He follows himself down the street in plate glass windows. He finds little interest in shopping for vegetables or shoes in open air. *They* look better to him behind plate glass (irony). This living doll (whom God cannot do enough for, and deservedly so!) (hyperbole) whines out a prayer (personification) for everybody else. He does not need it! *They* need it because *they* are intolerable (hyperbole). *They* need it because *they* are mean, low-down, egotistical jackasses (hyperbole expressed in metaphor). How sweet it is to be the innocent darling (litote).[50]

(3) Who is the stranger? (Rhetorical question.) The stranger sees himself in a strange land with a burning conviction that he is in touch with a transcendent realm of value.[51] He is the ground-covering guru of the small group (alliteration) who breezes into the local house church (anastrophe) (not to be confused with "church house") (parenthesis). He sees the subjects on the shag (alliteration) carpet looking upon him as knowing all, seeing all, hearing all (ellipsis). He seems to be up even when he sits down. In his talk he projects that he is the most honest, *the* most beneficent, *the* most humble (ellipsis). Even his silence commands the attention of the group. And his prayers command the attention of God who is told to listen carefully (personification). After he impresses the small group with his transcendental mystique, gazing eyes follow every step of his most benevolent excellence (hyperbole) to the outside. And they watch in wonder and awe as the *stranger* puts on his helmet, adjust his shades, slides onto his Honda and put-puts off into the darkness.

3. Now for a reflection upon the exercise we have just passed through: we can recount how we smiled or chuckled at some of the witty and ludicrous incongruities. And we can remember too well the pondersome task of reading the ontological comments *explaining* the humor. What little humor might have been expressed in the part of speech was wiped

away by the explanation. *Jokes cannot be explained* and re-*main funny* unless one makes a joke out of explaining a joke. But try and explain *that* joke and the joke is on you! "The correct explanation of a joke not only does not sound funny, but it does not sound like a correct explanation."[52] "In order to explain a thing you have to take it seriously; in order to feel humor you have to be playful. You cannot enjoy an explained joke for the same reason that you do not laugh when tickled by an ant, namely, the ant is serious and so are you."[53]

4. Humor reacts to incongruities within the ambiguities of life. Humor leaves when the incongruities are seen in the raw, when they are intellectualized in this ontology. But humor, a divine gift to see with truth incongruities, comes again through the next laugh, when we are again surprised by our glimpse of the "gap." When humor is evaluated, it no longer is laughable; a totally serious self is dealing with, of all things, the subject of humor.

Part II

ONTOLOGY OF HUMOR AND PHILOSOPHICAL THEOLOGY

In Part II we now see how the ontology of humor works within Christian experiences.

A. *Faith and Humor*

The limitless numbers of incongruities in human behavior leave one option for one's faith that is totally congruent and worthy of one's absolute trust. That object of one's faith is the truth that spotlights the gap that elicits the humor. The truth that reveals the incongruities in the same experience reveals that faith in that truth is the way to live within the countless ambiguities. Faith in anything else lends ultimate credibility to that limited, finite thing. And that remains faith in nothing. The many incongruities reveal nothing—and remain nothing until truth puts light on the situation and truly gives *being* to the human. That truth-illumined incongruity accepted by one gives being in spite of non-being.

Faith in truth gives true faith and frees one to have a sense of humor. "In true faith the ultimate concern is a concern about the truly ultimate; while in idolatrous faith preliminary, finite realities are elevated to the rank of ultimacy."[54] This ultimate concern for truth shatters idolatrous faith in finite realities. For instance, when the finite concern for racial supremacy is given the rank of ultimacy, only faith in the truth

37

can lift one above that finite "ultimacy" into the world of the truly ultimate, where *what is* really is and does not just seem to be. From that position of faith in truth (true faith) the lonely "ultimacy" of the finite concern breaks under the scrutiny of truth, and humor explodes the myth. Whites who believe that blacks have equal status in the United States have a difficult time keeping "straight" faces when they hear Muhammad Ali remind them of their vocabulary: "The Angel Food Cake is white; the Devil's Food Cake is dark brown. The President lives in the *White House*. It's all right to tell a *white* lie! If you don't do right, boy, you'll be *black* listed!" That truth spoken spotlights the incongruities, elicits the humor, and destroys the finite concern of racial supremacy that had been given ultimate concern.

> This is not a theoretical problem of the kind of higher or lower evidence of probability or improbability, but it is an existential problem of 'to be or not to be.' It belongs to a dimension other than any theoretical judgment. Faith is not belief, and it is not knowledge with a low degree of probability.[55]

The Ali illustration reveals that his faith in his worth as a human being works not in the arenas of theory, probability, or improbability but has to do with being or not being. His ultimate concern is to be somebody; in his words, "to be a man." His faith in the truth that he is a man opens to him a sense of the incongruities that would put him down. Instead, by the use of humor he puts down the shallow faith of the racial supremists in any society.

Faith in anything less than Truth creates an idolatrous faith, creates an incongruity by accepting *what is* not as if it were, and sets the stage for humor that destroys the idolatrous faith. Faith in truth saves, and humor is a part of that saving process.

B. *Faith Healing and Humor*

Faith healing, as the term is actually used, is the attempt

to heal others or oneself by mental concentration on the healing power in others or in oneself. There is such healing power in nature and man, and it can be strengthened by mental acts. In a nondepreciating sense one could speak of the use of magic power; and certainly there is healing magic in human relationships as well as in the relation to oneself. It is a daily experience and sometimes one that is astonishing in its intensity and success. But one should not use the word "faith" for it, and one should not confuse it with the integrating power of an ultimate concern.[56]

Where this understanding of faith prevails, there is no humor because there is no incongruity recognized. The power of healing is within the person. That power seriously asserts itself, and cannot laugh at itself in the healing process.

But when one sees faith as ultimate concern for Truth, this limited view of "faith" healing falls far short of healing that comes from faith that ultimately concerns itself with things beyond health of the body, beyond the finite. With that transcending faith view we cannot help but see humor in the professional faith healer on TV dressed in white suit, shoes, and tie, pink shirt, pocket handkerchief, and socks, with his tuxedoed helpers who catch those who receive the laying on of hands and are knocked unconscious by the experience. The subjects may actually be healed of a peptic ulcer, but the bruises gained from the healing can mar the whole experience. Attempting to pass such antics (that do heal in some cases) as the healing that comes from ultimate concern comes off as ludicrous. For instance, these professional faith healers will not lay their credibility on the line by choosing to heal a 97-year-old man of blindness. They know he is too close to death's door to bother with. They try to pass their "faith" healing off as the ultimate, to be doing something they are not doing, to be someone they are not. The obvious incongruity under Truth calls for humor.

But now, let us go to faith as this ontology understands it. We have seen how faith in Truth (when our ultimate concern is Truth) gives one a sense of humor. This means that humor becomes a healing by-product of faith.

> Faith . . . does not mean the belief in assertions for which there is no evidence. It never meant that in genuine religion, and it never should be abused in this sense. But faith means being grasped by a power that is greater than we are, a power that shakes us and turns us, and transforms us and heals us. Surrender to this power is faith. The people whom Jesus could heal and can heal are those who did do this self-surrender to the healing power in Him. They surrendered their persons, split, contradicting themselves, disgusted and despairing about themselves, hateful of themselves and therefore hostile towards everybody else; afraid of life, burdened with guilt feelings, accusing and excusing themselves, fleeing from others into loneliness, fleeing from themselves to others, trying finally to escape from the threats of existence into the painful and deceptive safety of mental and bodily disease.[57]

Our incongruities reveal our contradicting selves. At this sight we may show toward ourselves disgust, despair, hate, fear, guilt, etc. because we take ourselves too seriously. Humor, a look at these same negatives with Truth, breaks up the seriousness toward ourselves and in the process loosens the hold of all these emotions against ourselves. That in itself starts the healing process. When Jesus healed the disintegrated man at Gedara, it is conceivable (it is hardly conceivable any other way) that the first reaction of the wretched man was to laugh. That would have marked an obvious break from his sordid past. Jesus said, "Know the truth and the truth will make you free." [58] Truth frees one to laugh (nobody uptight can laugh), to conquer despair, fear, and all other negatives; leaves no reasons to escape into the dis-eases of sickness; and gives one a sense of wholeness.

We know that the human body is born into the dying process. Humor glimpses the gaps, heals the splits, conquers the pain. Humor helps us to die healthy.

C. *The Real, Fantasy, and Humor*

In Part I we discussed how the gap that exists between what is and what ought to be elicits humor. The negative side of the gap we call realism; the positive side, idealism. It is when we accept the negative as if it were the positive, the realism as if it were idealism, the imperfect as if it were perfect, the finite as if it were infinite, the "is" as if it were the "ought," when we imagine an incongruity within non-being, that we create fantasy. Now comes a fantasized "real" world. Beyond that fantasized "realism" still stands what ought to be, while the negative side of the gap remains fantasized realism. "Men faint, falling from the height of their moral goodness and youthful power, and just when they have fallen and are weakest, they run without weariness and rise up with wings as eagles. God acts beyond all human assumptions and valuations." [59] Being-itself always gives forth what ought to be no matter where man assumes or values himself to be. Fantasized realism makes it inevitable that men fall from their height of moral goodness. Humor through a glimpse of the gap can be one way to soften the fall. Fantasies bombard us from every quarter: from institutions such as governments and churches; from revolutionaries who claim a utopia. A sense of incongruities in these forms of fantasized "realisms" comes from God's Truth. "He gives power to the faint and their strength is renewed, so that they shall mount up with wings as eagles." [60] One way He does this is through humor. A good sense of humor changes the weak into the strong and gives power to the faint. It lifts one above the "real" world into God's order. This interplay between what is and what ought to be, between the earthbound order and the eternal order, continues to and through the end of this finite existence. Good humor remains God's way of helping us cope with the fantasies and "mount up with wings as eagles."

D. *Courage and Humor*

Humor helps one discover courage. The put-on bravado, when one acts like what he is not, shows that what commonly

41

passes itself off as courage is under truth the non-being side of the gap that elicits humor. That non-being side of the gap that elicits humor can also be seen in one's trying to will his courage to be, in trying to create his courage. The classic example of whistling in the dark illustrates this futile effort of the self trying to create courage. That non-being side of the gap can also be seen in man's discovery of courage in himself. His expression concerning his discovery sounds more braggadocious than courageous, and therefore humorous.

Humor reveals one not as one ought to be if one is to be courageous and points to courage in its unmasking false courage as something one possesses. In its exposure of the incongruity, humor points to a courage that possesses the person. Courageous people do not know they are. If they "know" they are, it is egotism, not courage. One does not control courage; courage controls the person. Being-itself coaxes the self to "come out" and be in spite of the threat of non-being expressed in anxiety. When one steps out and affirms one self, that expression of one's being is courage. That courageous state of one's being comes with all the risks involved. Without the risks as manifestations of the threats of non-being courage could not be. Even in despair one has enough being to allow the possibility of despair in the first place. One can only feel bad when one feels good enough to feel bad. Courage as self-affirmation works out of all levels of the threats of non-being. There is no humor in these expressions of courage.

Not only does humor help discover the condition of courage, but humor works to challenge one's courage continually, to point to the incongruities of those acting courageously. It takes courage *to be* loving. Love risks. It takes courage to free one loved to love in return. Humor stands by to point its finger at the false love of possessiveness. For example, you laugh as a husband says to his wife: "I love you so much that I can't ever let you out of my sight."

It takes courage *to be* forgiving because first we have to be forgiven. It seems easier to justify our actions. But those reasons that justify our wrongs are non-existent, non-being.

Those imagined self-justified reasons cause us not to be. We can be when we have the courage to admit who we are, what we've done wrong, and what we want: forgiveness. Humor that comes from the incongruities of one's acting as if he is forgiving points to the missing element—courage: "I forgive you, but I'll never forget what you've done to me." The courage to forgive erases the incongruity. The absence of humor in this instance means that the courage is genuine.

However, in those conditions of courage humor may still be available and practiced by the one possessed by courage. One possessed by courage finds oneself able to laugh at self and other's incongruities.

One possessed by courage finds himself able to see incongruities in other areas of his life, face the truth, admit his errors, close the gap, and go on to face other incongruities in life. Courage then restores a sense of humor and defeats non-being by laughing at the meaninglessness of non-being, by seeing how ridiculous it is to try to make meaninglessness meaningful—to mistake non-being for being. Mistaking non-being for being leads to strange conclusions and actions; for example, some well-meaning people preach that once we understand the causes of terrorism we might even be supportive of their programs. In one instance we know of, church offerings were used to support the terrorists in Zimbabwe. That same logic is being used to support terrorist actions in other parts of the world.

The courage to laugh at this non-being masked as being reduces its meaning to what it truly is: a meaningless nothing. Imagine a free-will offering taken: "On this occasion let us take a free-will offering that will allow us to buy medicines for those terrorists who might be injured following a bombing raid on innocent children riding a school bus."

Humor reduces non-being to a powerlessness and senselessness that shows non-being *is not*. It can no longer stand as being. Laughter destroys the power of non-being. Humor exposes the powerlessness of meaninglessness. This humor remains a meaningful act of courage.

"Being, limited by non-being, is finitude. Non-being ap-

43

pears as the 'not yet' of being and the 'no more' of being. It confronts that which is with a definite end (*Finis*)." [61] Courage to accept that nothingness as "part" of our being in finitude is the only way to deal with this constant threat of nothingness.

E. *"Born Again" and Humor*

While "born again" Christians should of all people be possessed of good humor, many are devoid of it and in that proud stance render themselves unintended comics. The ontology of humor calls for, in fact demands, humor to be in the new experience of faith. (Look at writings "Faith and Humor" and "Justification and Humor" in Part II of this book.)

> The use of the word "experience," however does not imply that he who is grasped by the Spiritual Presence can verify his experience through empirical observation. Though born anew, men are not yet new beings but have entered a new reality which can make them into new beings. Participating in the New being does not automatically guarantee that one is new.[62]

The common mistake of "born again" Christians rises out of their conscious efforts to look redeemed. This makes for humor in a ludicrous manner and calls for a re-evaluation on the part of the "born again" witnesses. Ontologically one *beg*ins to participate in a new awareness. One never thought that way before. Where life once never offered much (heavy on the non-being), now there is purpose (being). The awareness that God matters most (Being-itself stands behind all this) is sufficient evidence that one is born again. Anything more is self-induced and casts unreal images, which the "born again" expect all to live. The temptation to expect everybody to come through "the experience" acting alike and talking alike overcomes the weak in the faith and causes endless inconsistencies and contradictions. This writer knows some of these "born again" who set patterns that make others' actions unacceptable. One family will not permit their children to attend dances. Another not only permits their children to go to dances but pays for their dancing lessons. Another finds a way to "push the ox in the ditch" and work on Sunday, while another would not be caught in such an obviously un-Christian action. He would rather watch football on TV! While all these inconsistencies and incongruities take place, the "born again" are still that: they are born again into a new awareness that God guides their destiny, that God knows best, does the best, is the best—that God *is!*

This awareness lived out in one's life re-creates one into a new being. It carries all the power one needs *to be* and carries with it the power to see the incongruities that make for the comic in many of those born again—the power of Truth. When the "born again" act like they have *got it* as nobody else does, as if they were old-pros in their understanding, the Truth stands ready to spotlight that incongruity, trigger the humor, close the gap, and set them straight with their experience. Now they know God, Who gives their life meaning and a deep sense of well-being. Now they are a new being beginning.

F. *Justification and Humor*

Some of a person's most comic incongruities arise from one's efforts to justify one's actions. A constant justifying of actions in order to make sure one is never caught in a mistake turns out to be the biggest mistake of all. That turns out some hilarious humor. This effort of trying to do something we cannot do implies we think we are something we are not. This is the incongruity.

This humor helps us see the futility of all efforts of self-justification and urges us to look to another source for justification. That source is God's grace. Faith is the receiving act, and this act is itself a gift of grace.

> Therefore one should dispense completely with the phrase "justification by faith" and replace it by the

45

formula "justification by grace through faith." It should be a serious concern in the teaching and preaching of every minister that this profound distortion of the "good news" of the Christian gospel be remedied.[63]

Without grace faith becomes *our* faith. Without grace faith falls more in the category of works and makes for but another effort of self-justification. Truth shines on one who, by intellectual prowess, proves his faith with an air of justification that can come only from the self. Truth also shines on *what* is taking place, shines out of God's grace. Truth reflects Being-itself being itself, reflects on where one ought to be within that grace. In that gap between how one acts justified and who one needs *to be* (in God's grace) lies humor. Beyond the look at that gap lies a sublime sense of well-being, the experience of justifying grace through faith.

G. *Enthusiasm and Humor*

Contrary to popular belief, enthusiasm is anything but the ultimate virtue. Enthusiasm as commonly experienced offers a field day in the study of humor. Every passionate support of an idea, a value, a tendency, a human being, any *thing* gives that object the status of a god, and under the illumination of Truth reveals a world of humor. To illustrate: During a presidential election year in America if a flag-waving, button-wearing Republican or Democrat should die and go to Heaven, she/he would expect St. Peter to take a back seat and let a clone of his/her candidate open the Pearly Gates. Another illustration: At one of our Rotary Clubs the fellow who leads us in singing the national anthem (or "America") and the Pledge to the Flag bounces, announces, grins, and literally shakes with enthusiasm. His overexcitment leaves us fatigued and out of breath. The only thing that keeps us from getting "out of sorts" is a glimpsing grin with the fellow across the table.

Ultimate concern given to any *thing* generates enthusiasm —and humor—because we are *not* who we ought to be.

Thing in this sense is anything created. When one's ultimate concern is given to the Creator of all things, that joining up lends itself not to humor but to ecstacy. However, when that ecstacy solidifies into doctrine, the resulting overexcitement becomes expected by adherents to the experience. Rather than being grasped by Being-itself (ecstacy), they try to grasp the ecstacy. The resulting humor is ludicrous as Truth spotlights this "spiritual" incongruity.

H. *Goodness and Humor*

Man's sense of goodness makes for much of the humor in man. About the best man can come up with is *half*-goodness because tacked onto every good he can dream up or do is an ulterior motive, be it ever so subtle as, "I'll show you I'm as good as anybody you know." So many of our incongruities are made up of our showing off what we see as our *good* qualities. (In Part I we have dealt with this as *hubris*). The "spiritual X-ray" powers of Truth in humans *being* open to Truth can spot these show-off *goodies* in humanity. They are far more comic than the antics of bad people (the bad as non-being offers within itself no incongruity). Good people, by looking in on their own goodness, offer themselves no opportunity to see the negative side of the incongrity exposed by Truth.

A humorous look at the incongruities of our *good* with the help of Truth can be a good experience if we go beyond that glimpse of our incongruities to Good-itself, to Being-itself.

> If God accepted him who is half-sinner and half-just, his judgment would be conditioned by man's half-goodness. But there is nothing God rejects as strongly as half-goodness and every human claim based on it. The impact of this message, mediated by the Spiritual Presence, turns the eyes of many away from the bad and the good in themselves to the infinite divine goodness, which is beyond good and bad and which gives itself without conditions and ambiguities. . . . The courage to surrender

one's own goodness to God is the central element in the courage of faith.[64]

I. *Joy and Humor*

One's being in Being-good-itself remains for one: God is good, and it is good to know it. God's goodness saves us from our own sense of goodness. In this salvation operation humor plays a large part and remains a gift of the Spirit. The saved person is not the humored good person but the good humored person who knows the One from whom good comes.

Humor about one's self shatters the heaviness of oppressive sternness and *can* lead to joy if one is willing to go beyond the laugh. That step beyond humor that leads to joy comes when one realizes what one has going for one, when one accepts that the Truth that exposes the incongruity also accepts one who remains a mixture of ambiguities. That acceptance gives one a deep sense of sublime oneness with the power of Being-itself. It gives joy, the knowing of Truth and beauty, the experience beyond one's incongruities—beyond humor.

> Joy is possible only when we are driven towards things and persons because of what they are and not because of what we can get from them. The joy about our work is spoiled when we perform it not because of what we produce but because of the pleasures with which it can provide us, or the pain against which it can protect us. The pleasure about the fact that *I* am successful spoils the joy about the success itself. Our joy about knowing truth and experiencing beauty is spoiled if we enjoy not the truth and the beauty but the fact that it is *I* who enjoy them.[65]

When one begins to talk about anything enjoyed as if it were one's own possession, that joy turns to pleasure and thus returns to the world of humor. To illustrate: As a rooster crows because the sun has risen just for him, a husband looks and

48

acts the same way when his wife enters the room. In his mind he is the head kingpin; in her mind he is the king pin head! This comic stands in the quicksand of incongruities as he relishes his pleasures. He goes beyond his pleasures to the experiences of joy when he sees his ridiculous *cockeyed* stance, laughs at himself, accepts the Truth that exposes his incongruities—that reveals the beauty of his wife. In that experience one transcends his incongruities and for a time knows joy. This ecstasy cannot remain his experience. His incongruities in other areas will surely snatch him back into his humorous world.

J. *Love, Grace, and Humor*

Love provides humor. That spirit of love arises out of the experience of Being-itself. Anyone who feels as if he is somebody knows truly the experience of love. A sense of incongruities, especially one's own, brings about a sense of wellbeing when one accepts the truth that elicits the humor. That acceptance of truth in faith is the experience of love. One who loves truth cannot help but be open to good humor. Find a person without a sense of love, and you find a person without a sense of humor. One can give forth with love after one has experienced the Truth that shows in humor who one is and who one ought to be. When one accepts who one ought to be, that acceptance brings forth a sense of well-being. That is love; that love *is*.

> Love is also the motivating power in theonomous morality. We have seen the ambiguities of the law's demanding obedience—even if it is the law of love. Love is ambiguous, not as law, but as grace. Theologically speaking, Spirit, love, and grace are one and the same reality in different aspects. Spirit is the creative power; love is its creation; grace is the effective presence of love in man."[66]

The love that provides humor is not love as law but love as Grace. Love as law introduces an oughtness into the situation and fulfills that particular function of love as Grace. Ambi-

49

guities arise out of man's efforts to abide by the law of love. In seminary I had a theology professor who personified this ambiguity. One day in a seminar without warning he asked what was the motivating force behind good works. Unhappy with the delayed response, he shouted while pounding his fist on the table, "It's love, dammit, it's love!" No doubt he felt he was promoting love in his tirade against classroom silence. The ambiguities that arise out of trying to keep the law of love also furnish a world of incongruities. No one laughed at the professor in the classroom. We were too close to the subject for it to be humorous! Outside, we laughed at the incongruity of the professor who preached one thing while acting out another.

There are as many ways of trying to keep the law of love, to do what we ought to do, as there are people and situations of interplay between people that constantly change. And every effort under the scrutiny of Truth furnishes incongruities that make for humor. For instance, the law of love says, "Tell the truth." In that quest some folks tell everything they have ever done or thought wrong. This display of "honesty" makes them feel as if they have kept the law of love. The enjoyment of telling about all their sins robs them of the accomplishment of love. They are still not as they ought to be. And humor prevails.

The incongruities arising out of efforts to keep the law of love can be overcome when we keep the law of love because we *are kept* by love as grace. Now love becomes unambiguous, and the gaps of incongruities close because the total act belongs to God, to Being-itself. In Him we live and move and have our being. "Sin is estrangement; grace is reconciliation. Precisely because God's reconciling grace is unconditional, man does not need to look at his own condition and the degrees of his guilt. He has the certainty of total forgiveness in the situation of total guilt."[67] Love as grace carries its own weight. It just *is*. One can know this when one knows that all efforts to make oneself keep the law of love have failed. Even in one's failure, one is accepted. That love as grace reconciles man to God. Man will always strive to keep the law of love

50

and will be ludicrous in his actions. He must strive. His finer moments come when he knows beyond his efforts that God loves, forgives, and accepts anyway. That sublime awareness does not have humor in it.

K. *"Wrath of God" and Humor*

By its ontological nature a sense of humor remains a sure sign of the providential presence of God. One has to be in touch with Truth in order to see the incongruities that elicit humor. By virtue of that relationship (seeing and knowing with Truth) one escapes the wrath of God.

> "The wrath of God is neither a divine effect alongside his love nor a motive for action alongside providence; it is the emotional symbol for the work which rejects and leaves to self-destruction what resists it. The experience of the wrath of God is the awareness of the self-destructive nature of evil, namely, of those acts and attitudes in which the finite creature keeps itself separated from the ground of being and resists God's reuniting love. Such an experience is real, and the metaphorical symbol "the wrath of God" is unavoidable."[68]

Humor does not reject or resist love but depends on it (see section above on Love, Grace, and Humor). Humor lends itself to self-fulfillment (see later section on Self-transcendence, and Humor), thereby avoiding the self-destructive nature of evil. Humor can only be recognized with Truth that arises out of the ground of being. This leaves no place for "the wrath of God" in humor. (The exception is sick humor, which is not humor since it exemplifies nothingness.)

Look what this ontological understanding of "the wrath of God" in relation to humor does to the typical condemnation offered by people on behalf of God's wrath. We have all been subjected to the hyper-judgmental fanatic who tells us we are going to hell and smiles as she/he says it. Anyone who puts oneself up as dispenser of God's wrath has put oneself where one does not belong. The position is groundless. There

51

is nothing to what is said. It is fantasy. That judgmental person has unwittingly placed himself/herself in a negative position relative to the God of love and thus receives "the wrath of God" that he/she had so authoritatively pronounced on others. One can never be as far from God as when one claims to be the dispenser of His wrath.

One way to save a judgmental one from this "wrath of God" comes through humor. A willingness to glimpse with Truth that we *are not* the mouthpiece for God's wrath, that we are the mouthpiece of nothing, that we ought to stand in unity with divine love, and love whether people respond or not. A look at that gaping incongruity offers the judgmental person an escape from "the wrath of God." That laugh at oneself truly would be a Godsend, an invitation *to be* saved, *to be* loving even when our expressions of love are rejected.

L. *Guilt and Humor*

"It is possible to distinguish 'essential' finitude from 'existential' disruption, ontological anxiety from the anxiety of guilt which is despair."[69] Essential finitude has been seen in the baby who experiences "nothing" (non-being) as he/she struggles through his/her rudimentary crises (ontological anxiety) toward freedom. That is *healthy* non-being. Existential disruption is *healthy* non-being thrown into disarray by the anxiety of guilt which is despair. When guilt takes over, the non-being of finitude becomes nightmarish in its effect on a person. We have seen how humor works in finitude through the baby's laughter at the bottle of orange juice that is and then is not. That incongruity triggers the humor. Should that baby grow into adulthood and be invited to the Alfred Hitchcock dinner party where all are served an entire meal dyed blue, that surprise incongruity would remain humor within essential finitude. Should a member of that party become inebriated and kill someone in a car wreck en route home, the outcome for him would be existential disruption, a despairing-guilt anxiety. There is no humor within guilt anxiety. However, humor remains a potential for one in the des-

52

pair of guilt. Non-being has not totally overshadowed one's being. One at least still remains someone who is. As long as one *is*, incongruities are possible. The stronger one *be*comes, the greater the return of incongruities. (There are no incongruities in non-being). Because guilt does allow room for some incongruities to emerge, humor may still occur though considerably squelched. While one may sense humor in other areas, there is no humor concerning his guilt. If humor concerning one's guilt ever occurs, it will come after forgiveness, a restored sense of self-worth, a condition of being that is *given* by Being-itself. Only then can humor be used about one's past guilt if the time, place, and distance removed from the despair are adequate.

M. *Doubt and Humor*

"Emptiness and loss of meaning are expressions of the threat of non-being to the spiritual life. This threat is implied in man's finitude and actualized by man's estrangement. It can be described in terms of doubt, its creative and its destructive function in man's spiritual life."[70] While *healthy* non-being remains essential in finitude, it threatens one as existential anxiety. This threat may come in the form of doubt, a doubt that can lead to creative functions in finitude. On this level doubt may be a means of healthy humor. It's mood reflects the not-so, the negative dimension that creates the surprise or that keeps the constant off-beat expressions of the ludicrous alive. A methodological look can evaluate the incongruities caused by this doubt (and the humor leaves as reasoning takes over).

This doubt that can help trigger the awareness of the incongruity in finitude becomes destructive in estrangement—when one is emptied into the abyss of meaninglessness. "If the awareness of not having has swallowed the awareness of having, doubt has ceased to be methodological asking and has become existential despair."[71] There is no humor in this situation, no recognized incongruity because the "not having" has swallowed the awareness of "having." This total *not-ness* leaves not enough of the self, of being, to recognize life's incongruities. As the despair of truth becomes complete, not enough awareness of truth remains that can see with Truth life's incongruities.

But humor remains a potential way out for one caught in existential despair caused by doubt, as long as an attempt is not made to make something humorous out of that despair! This would only deepen the existential anxiety because there are no incongruities in non-being (only imaginary ones that make up sick humor). Humor comes later in the process of conquering doubt. The initial phases of conquering doubt come when one strains to find meaning, to find some authority that can give one meaning, to do anything to keep from taking the risk of asking and doubting. The resulting fanatical self-assertiveness now creates a picture of incongruity with stark clarity by objectifying the anxiety it was supposed to conquer. This cover-up offers a contrast, a contradiction, an incongruity. It shows blatantly how one acts like what he is not. Transcending Truth spotlights that incongruity. If one sees this (even in someone else), one has the opportunity of seeing the humor. That humor can restore one to one's finite anxiety—to risk asking and doubting once again. That humor becomes the acceptance of despair that "is in itself faith and on the boundary line of the courage to be."[72]

N. *Prayer and Humor*

A prominent attorney-at-law at the 8:05 A.M. men's prayer time (program called "The Twelve") said in the beginning sentence: "It seems almost ludicrous that I can pray asking for anything—I have so much."

He was right. All prayers are ludicrous when the one who prays does all the talking.

> Every serious and successful prayer—which does not talk to God as a familiar partner, as many prayers do—is a speaking to God, which means that God is made into an object for him who prays. However, God can never be an object, unless He is a subject at the same time. We **can only pray to the God who prays to Himself through**

us. Prayer is a possibility only insofar as the subject-object structure is overcome; hence, it is an ecstatic possibility. Herein lies both the greatness of prayer and the danger of its continuous profanization."[73]

The subject-object prayer model in itself is ludicrous. Imagine the *hubris* of one who prays to God as if God were an object! It is a funny sight that shows prayer is not as it ought to be. A glimpse of that incongruity can be the beginning of a vital prayer life. First, it can open one to listen to God in prayer, to let the power of God's Being come in and make one feel one *is* accepted, *is* somebody. Then one becomes in this relationship with God *to be* in the spirit of prayer. Out of that spirit one may or may not talk, but one will always be *with it*. One may moan, shout for joy, cry; and as long as one is in the spirit of prayer, one may "pray to God" with the assurance that God was there before a word was spoken.

To see the ludicrous in our prayer life could lead to a helpful awakening in our devotional life. In that time-set-aside one would do well to use a good portion of time reflecting with Truth (with God) at one's incongruities in prayer life, in all of life. Then when the time came to pray to God, one could know that God's spirit guides one in that prayer to Him. One would sublimely feel that God was talking through prayer with Himself. One's being would be immersed in Being-itself.

0. *Miracles and Humor*

The experience of a miracle helps one live with a sense of humor.

A genuine miracle is first of all an event which is astonishing, unusual, shaking, without contradicting the rational structure of reality. In the second place, it is an event which points to the mystery of being, expressing its relation to us in a definite way. In the third place, it is an occurrence which is received as a sign-event in an ecstatic experience. Only if these three conditions are fulfilled can one speak of a genuine miracle. That which

55

does not shake one by its astonishing character has no revelatory power. That which shakes one without pointing to the mystery of being is not miracle but sorcery. That which is not received in ecstasy is a report about the belief in a miracle, not an actual miracle. This is emphasized in the synoptic records of the miracles of Jesus. Miracles are given only to those for whom they are sign-events, to those who receive them in faith. Jesus refuses to perform "objective" miracles. They are contradictions in terms. This strict correlation makes it possible to exchange the words describing miracles and those describing ecstasy. One can say that ecstasy is the miracle of the mind and that miracle is the ecstasy of reality." [74]

With Paul Tillich's definition of miracle in mind we can see first of all that one who is in a state of astonishment at the unusual within a miracle cannot sense incongruities. The second criterion of a miracle points to the mystery of being in a personal way. That relation with Being-itself leaves us swallowed up by the mystery. Being-itself accepts all our contradictions, inconsistencies, and incongruities and, in so doing, renders them powerless to produce humor. The third criterion sees the miracle as a sign-event in an ecstatic experience. A look at what this means quickly does away with any opportunity for humor within the experience of the miraculous.

As ecstacy presupposes the shock of non-being in the mind, so sign-events presuppose the stigma of non-being in the reality. In shock and stigma, which are strictly correlated, the negative side of the mystery of being appears. . . . There is a stigma that appears on everything, the stigma of finitude, or implicit and inescapable non-being. It is striking that in many miracle stories there is a description of the 'numinous' dread which grasps those who participate in the miraculous events. There is the feeling that the solid ground of ordinary reality is taken 'out from under' their feet. The correlative experience of the stigma of non-being in the reality and the shock of non-being in the mind produces this feeling, which,

56

although not revelatory in itself, accompanies every genuine revelatory experience."[75]

The ontological shock of non-being is never funny.

Although humor does not come in the experience of a miracle, the experience of a miracle may bring humor to life by permitting one to see reality. Over against the realities of non-being/being within the miracle the accepted norms of life begin more and more to look like fantasies. The miracle as a bringer of Truth becomes the light that shines on incongruities and elicits the humor. The experience of a miracle in all its soul-shaking dimensions leaves an indelible mark on the recipient. That experience creates the truly serious-minded person, gives that one the sense not to take oneself and all one's human contradictions so seriously, and gives that one a sense of humor. Miracles then give people the ability to see the humorous.

P. *Individual/Collective and Humor*

"Life individualizes in all its forms; at the same time, mutual participation of being in 'being' maintains the unity of being."[76] One cannot objectify the total being of mankind in order to see a clear-cut incongruity. The reason for this comes from the millions of individual human *beings*. Only a caricature of humanity, the individualization of the collective may provide the incongruity that evokes humor. For example, a new year's cartoon shows the New Year baby in its diaper playing in its play pen with the Grim Reaper's sword. This evokes nervous laughter and requires no caption.

Another reason one cannot objectify the collective comes from one's inability, inherent in one's estrangement from self and others, to objectify anything. How can one objectify anything one is estranged from? One's inherent subjectivity arises out of one's estrangement. That subjectivity expresses itself through self-centered attitudes and values. One's efforts to objectify out of this fault/broken ground of estrangement remains subjective. One becomes intensely wrapped up in one's "objective" evaluation. This makes one's best effort at objectifying merely one's best exercise at subjectivity. This dilemma is solved only when truth illumines the object and the person (the subject) sees with truth the object. These are those times (kairoi) one knows the truth. But one never knows all the truth about anything at any time. Humor remains one sure way one may know one is being objective. By way of illustration: the little fellow about to get on the witness stand is asked the impossible: "Do you swear to tell the truth, the whole truth, nothing but the truth, so help you God?" And he answers, "Yes." The only experience of objectivity comes in that moment of truth which reveals the incongruity. The fellow swore to God that he would tell the "whole truth" when he could hardly find his way to the witness stand. Humor then remains a moment of true objectivity amidst the condition of estrangement.

There are few (if any) recognized incongruities in man *in general* (corporate). An intensely academic mind might see a cosmic humor concerning corporate man. But even then the likelihood is that corporate man would be viewed as a stereotype. And a stereotype has the *individual* look. Humor then is seen in individuals or in *individual* images.

Q. Knowledge (Absolutism/Relativism) and Humor

Absolutism/relativism eludes empiricism. One cannot finally see precise relativism. If anything is absolute, it is that observation! Because it is truth. We can never know all about anything. And that is the truth. That is absolute. What we know is not relative to the truth but relative to our finite capabilities to translate the absolute truth.

> Knowledge of reality has never the certitude of complete evidence. The process of knowing is infinite. It never comes to an end except in a state of knowledge of the whole. But such knowledge transcends infinitely every finite mind and can be ascribed only to God. Every knowledge of reality by the human mind has the charac-

ter of higher or lower probability. The certitude about a physical law, a historical fact, or a psychological structure can be so high that, for all practical purposes, it is certain. But theoretically the incomplete certitude of belief remains and can be undercut at any moment by criticism and new experience."[77]

A new experience that undercuts a belief in a set of facts can be humor. When one is so sure of one's facts, so certain that what one knows is absolute, what is "out there" is "out there" just exactly as one says it is "out there," one has lifted oneself into God's place. Only Being-itself knows what is. That is God's nature. Facts are ideas in man's mind. Being-itself does not deal in man's facts but transcends all facts, all the highest of probabilities in man's mind, by being the Truth. That transcending truth shines above and beyond all claimers to the facts and spotlights their incongruities. Anybody who acts as if his/her interpretation of the truth is truth itself comes off comic. Sometimes tragically comic! For instance, on the religious/political scene everybody has his own set of facts. Iran's Khomeini claims he knows the mind of God and kills those who have sinned against God. He feels justified in this killing. He has the facts against the sinners! He is a clown with the power to destroy.

When they told us that the flat earth was round, we accepted these facts. Then the facts were that the earth was pear-shaped. We laughed because that sounded a bit ludicrous because we knew that pears looked more like people than earth. Now the space pictures show the earth to be a fairly well-rounded "pear." Every day somebody comes up with more facts. He does not know it, but he has set the stage for a laugh as later facts do him in. Man's claim to knowledge makes him the funniest creature on earth.

R. *The Law and Humor*

While keeping the law is what one ought to *do*, a keeper of the law is not necessarily what one ought to *be*. Because one is not what one ought to be, one must have law that one ought to keep. When one keeps the law, one is keeping oneself from doing what by nature one would like to do but ought not. By keeping the law, by not doing what one would like to do, one is not what one ought to be on the inside. Further, this effort itself means that one is not who he ought to be while he may do what he ought to do.

The "ought" in doing and the "ought" in being come from the same source—Being-itself. "Freedom from the law is the power to judge the given situation in the light of the Spiritual Presence and to decide upon adequate action, which is often in seeing contradiction to the law."[78] The "ought-to-be" is essential to one's being. It calls one to do what he ought to do. This conflict-in-action calls for humor when one is not what he ought to be but tries to look like it. To illustrate: A groceryman said to a young boy standing near the apple bin, "Son, are you trying to steal those apples?" "No, sir," answered the boy, "I'm trying *not* to!"

S. *Authority and Humor*

Heteronomous authority from outside puts pressure on the self divided against itself. This authority tries to force out incongruities, tries to close the gap, tries to maintain congruity. This kind of authority does not accomplish congruity but takes on the look of congruity, i.e., people *look* law-abiding, *look* as if they *are* following the commands of parents, *look* as if they are following orders. Heteronomous authority sets people up for humor. It makes them act like something they are not.

If one can laugh at his looks in response to heteronomous authority, one may find in return a bearable heteronomy.

Autonomous authority comes from within. It assumes power of the self. When autonomous power tries to force one's incongruities out of the self, or when one assumes that one has succeeded in pulling himself together into a fully congruent self, humor results.

These self-making efforts serve only to open wide another gap in the self. This ingrown authority reveals the weakness of the self in its *show* of strength.

Again, if one can laugh at a person's efforts to save himself, autonomous authority loses its power to delude the self into thinking it has power it does not have.

Theonomous authority is the only authority that has the power to close the gap. It does this through Truth, the only power that reveals the incongruity and closes the gap. This authority cannot be laughed at but retains the power to elicit the incongruities. This authority is the only real authority. All other finally fails because the self never reaches its best self except under theonomous authority.

T. *Revelation, History, and Humor*

> There is no reality, thing, or event which cannot become a bearer of the mystery of being and enter into a revelatory correlation. Nothing is excluded from revelation in principle because nothing is included in it on the basis of special qualities. No person and no thing is worthy in itself to represent our ultimate concern. On the other hand, every person and every thing participates in Being-itself, that is, in the ground and meaning of being. Without such participation it would not have the power of being. This is the reason why almost every type of reality has become a medium of revelation somewhere."[79]

Truth spotlights the incongruity, and thus humor becomes another reality revealed. The experience of the incongruity *with* the Truth of Being-itself *reveals* the humor. This makes the humor a revelation rather than a deductive reasoning experience. In fact, deductive reasoning destroys the humor revealed. Any effort to explain the humor explains it away. Humor then is reasonable in the sense that it makes its own sense. It is a revealed sensibility.

Many incongruities are revealed by the truth of Being-itself in any one time/space frame. These revealed incongruities are unreasonable by deductive reasoning, but knowable by different persons from their different perspectives *with* truth in the situation.

Humor is a revelation that plays a major role in history.

Incongruities in the world of people produce unlimited ambiguities. Historians are given the privilege of standing at a distance with Truth and viewing some of the larger incongruities participated in by the masses. For example, house painter Hitler saw himself as the master of a master race. For "history" Truth has spotlighted that incongruity.

"History never leaves the past, no matter how long ago 'it' happened. For Being-itself the past is not complete, because through it Being-itself creates the future; in creating the future, he re-creates the past. Past includes its own potentialities. The past changes through everything new that happens."[80] By their very nature incongruities are formed "between" two states of being. Those states may be years apart and recognized in a given moment. Since incongruities of past events are experienced in the *now*, any humorous reaction to them in the now changes the past, and that new interpretation of the past affects the future. For instance, men's long hair styles in the West were unacceptable in some Christian circles in the early 1970's. The hair length of Easterner Jesus Christ would be frowned on in some churches that bear His Name today. The awareness of that historical incongruity sets the stage for yet another historical incongruity when some colleges rejected the men's short hair styles! And now we see in the West men's hair short, long, and as much on the face as on the head. Our overreactions have thrown us into a mood of toleration. If this toleration turns into apathy, what will the hairlook of tomorrow turn into? We do not know. Yet we know it will never be the same because our changed ideas due to humorous interpretations of past incongruities spaced in history will make for a different future. These kinds of cultural incongruities are revealed by Truth simultaneously with the other general factors that determine the movement of history (e.g., economic, political, and educational). Essential to history is humor. Especially when we take our interpretation of history too seriously.

There is no static past. Interpretation will not permit it to "stay there."

We can never know what the event was. We merely have

our interpretation of it. Interpretations of the past change the future. Only God knows what is happening. He permits us to see some of what is happening in history when we see with His Truth man's incongruities, including our own— when we see with a sense of humor. This leads us to the existential dimension of all humor. For it to work, timing is essential.

U. *Finite/Infinite and Humor*

Not bound by time and space, Being-itself *is*. Within the bounds of time and space Being-itself also *is*. In all humorous situations time (timing) plays a large role. (One incongruity includes other incongruities). Many time events blend with many space events to make up what we see as *an* incongruity that makes for the laugh.

An ontic understanding of time reveals how a blend of many time/space events make up any given humorous situation. What we call time is a finite measurement of events in space. A hand on a clock jumps sixty times to go around the full circle. Each jump is an event that reveals a "distance" in space. The "distance" between these two events is what is called time. Take away any of these measurements in space and there is no time—only *now*, only is-ness. Many incongruities in time/space exist within the following incongruity (it reallp happened) and go to make up its *timings*: A preacher paid a visit to the widow's home within hours after her husband died. A crowd of sympathetic friends had already descended upon the house. Every room was filled with people. The pastor and his lady parishioner found themselves in the crowded hallway. The only place for privacy was in the bathroom off the hallway. The two found their way to that area where she sat on the side of the bathtub and he on the lid of the commode. After a time of counsel he said, "Let us bow for a *time* of prayer." They did. And when he completed the prayer with "Amen," he turned and flushed the commode. Later the pastor said, "It took an eternity for the water to flush." The surprise action triggered the incongruity:

commode flushing goes *not with* (non-being) prayer but with other experiences. Another incongruity existing within that time frame was the existing expectancy that this pastor could not make mistakes—he was so perfect. But he did, and it got funnier the more the people relived that incongruity (what they thought he thought he *was*, he *was not*). At the end of the same time/distance between when he flushed the toilet and when the water stopped, both the pastor and the widow burst into laughter—laughter that triggered frowns on the faces of those in the hallway nearby who couldn't see the humor when they heard about it. *They* tried to stay somber, the way they felt the situation *ought to be*. But what they thought *ought to be* came off as incongrous with the incongruity shared by the pastor and the widow. This made for ambiguity. Each person saw an incongruity from his/her own perspective. Some laughed; some did not. What was proper timing for one was not for another. From some angle within the same clock-time something was potentially humorous for somebody. Just as it is in all situations at all times.

V. *Self-transcendence and Humor*

Although humor takes place within the time/space dimension, the experience is non-spatial. That is, it is self-transcending. When the self (the "I am" awareness) is allowed a look with Truth at any incongruity within the self, that event in some way changes the self. In the process of self standing outside of self and seeing the incongruity of the self, the self transcends itself and to an extent is never the same again. In the humorous event one sees life differently, and that "look" will come back again on another occasion. The "I remember when . . . " reveals the never-ending influence of any event, including the humorous one, the process of self-transcendence.

Humor, as an experience of self-transcendence, can lead to self-evaluation without the self doing the evaluating. The truth that shines on the gap does the evaluating. The self either rejects or accepts that truth. A rejection puts self-transcendence in reverse. One becomes "more" of nothing than one once was. An acceptance of that truth pushes the self forward in a new being. A developed sense of one's own incongruities, a sense of humor concerning oneself, brings a stronger self out of the old self. Self-confidence is not a thing the self conjures up· for itself. Rather it is the self knowing the experience of Truth and loving it. When we go beyond the humor to Truth, we come out in the new self with confidence. If we do not go beyond the humor to the Truth that spotlights the incongruity, we go *no*where. Self-transcendence is stifled. If we do not go with Truth, we go in reverse. That leads to *no*where—to death of self.

One goes forward in self-transcendence when one accepts the Truth that shows the humor. So one must go beyond the humor to the Truth that makes humor possible. In accepting that Truth one progresses in one's maturity. At no point in this process of self-transcendence via humor does one become super-human. The "best" self is not a quality of the self. Rather the "best" self is the result of a self being in the Spirit of Truth. Humor, as an end in itself, is demonic because we have not accepted the truth that makes humor possible. God uses humor to call us out of our old selves *to be* in His Spirit of Truth.

W. *Freedom, Sanctification, and Humor*

A baby is born a reactionary (reacts to needs, e.g. sleep, food). Soon the child develops the ability to make choices. Then the person learns that choosing one's own destiny (with no outside interference) may lead to fame, riches, power, and death. The psychological/spiritual plunge comes in the twinkling of an eye. A consciousness of nothing (non-being) translates itself in words such as, "I feel like hell," or "I've nothing to live for," or "Nothing makes sense." These wrong choices make us prisoners of the self. The self is finite and temporary. Death inevitably results. On the other hand, choosing God's will brings freedom. We cannot know freedom until we know the Truth of God: "Know the truth and the truth will make you free." [81] And when we know the Truth, we know the power that spotlights the gaps and elicits the humor. Only in a state of freedom, then, can we see the humor. A free spirit senses incongruities. When we are imprisoned within our own selves, we see life "straight." When we are free under God's Truth, we can see incongruities, ours as well as others. This new-found freedom does not give serenity and protection from every disturbance. Quite the contrary, awareness of a magnitude undreamed comes with this freedom.

> Awareness of the element of "ought to be," and with its awareness of responsibility, guilt, despair, and hope, characterizes man's relation to the eternal. Everything temporal has a "teleological" relation to the eternal, but man alone is aware of it; and this awareness gives him the freedom to turn against it. The Christian assertion of the tragic universality of estrangement implies that every human being turns against his *telos*, against Eternal Life, at the same time that he aspires to it. [82]

This new awareness midst all the ambiguities of human existence includes the eye for humor. Freedom is essential to a sense of humor.

That freedom-oriented sense of incongruities paves the way for a truly sanctified life.

> Sanctification includes awareness of the demonic as well as the divine. Such awareness, which increases in the process of sanctification, does not lead to the Stoic "wise man," who is superior to the ambiguities of life because he has conquered his passions and desires, but rather to an awareness of these ambiguities in himself, as in everyone, and to the power of affirming life and its vital dynamics in spite of its ambiguities. [83]

This awareness of ambiguities that comes with freedom provides the glimpse of humor in the Stoic "wise man" who skillfully uses pliers to unscrew the safety cap of a medicine bottle. He acts like what he is not (he is not "above" being caught in the ambiguities of life). And the ludicrous erupts from the free spirit. "Freedom from the law in the process of sanctification is the increasing freedom from the commanding form of law." [84]

When we hear the call of sanctification in the imperative, i.e., "Be sanctified, be good, be holy," and we answer that command, all we can do is try to be holy and good. When we take our effort at holiness as if it *were* holiness, only freedom under Truth can release us from that death-hold on ourselves. And the release can come in a glimpse of that gap through humor.

Progress toward spiritual maturity (sanctification) can be judged by our sense of humor. We stymie our progression when we will not choose in accordance with the Truth that reveals incongruities midst all the ambiguities (see previous section on self-transcendence). Maturity comes, not as an accomplishment of character, but as a keener awareness of what is going on in the world, and a willingness to accept one's world the way Truth reveals it. That is sanctification accomplished in freedom lived out, and lived out to a large extent in humor. For example, a Holy Joe who gets in his mind an image of holiness and acts like that image comes off as ludicrous under Truth. A Holy Joe acting like that, who sees, under Truth, the incongruity of not being what he acts like, will now *become* a mature Holy Joe because now he sees he is not what he acts like and laughs at his feeble efforts *to be*. That laugh with Truth is maturity in the making and makes a sense of humor a sure sign of sanctification.

X. *The World and Humor*

What is meant by "world" in this section may be clarified in the following manner:

> If we call "world" the structured unity of an infinite manifoldness, personality and world may be understood as correlative concepts. Man alone has a world, while all living beings, including man, have an environment. But

67

man transcends any given environment in the power of the universal forms and structures of reality which make *him* a person and make the *whole of being* a world, a "cosmos." [85]

There is no humor in the world because as the multi-faceted expression of total being the world is sacred. A creation without incongruities. There is nothing to laugh at. The Truth that spotlights incongruities in the human acting *as he is* also reveals the essential being in the human, the *imago dei*, the oughtness that constantly keeps man becoming. That essential being that man knows in himself he also knows in all creation. There is a sacred order in the world.

This is as much as to say that religious man can live only in a sacred world, because it is only in such a world that he participates in being, that he has a *real existence*. This religious need expresses an unquenchable ontological thirst. Religious man thirsts for *being*. His terror of the chaos that surrounds his inhabited world corresponds to his terror of nothingness. The unknown space that extends beyond his world—an uncosmicized-unconsecrated space, a mere amorphous extent into which no orientation has yet been projected, and hence in which no structure has yet arisen—for religious man, this profane space represents absolute non-being. If, by some evil chance, he strays into it, he feels emptied of his ontic substance, as if he were dissolving in Chaos, and he finally dies.[86]

While religious man lives in a sacred world (the congruent world stays just that, sacred), that same man may be more "religious" than truly religious, than living as he *ought to be*. Only that kind of living, the *ought to be* sort, offers man his participation in total being, in the cosmos. When man's religious attitudes and actions thrust himself beyond the cosmos into the realm of the gods, his *hubris* perverts his participation in the world and makes the world "profane." His distortion does not change the sacredness of the world. He is able to distort, indeed, because the world is sacred! There may be distortions of the distortions, but somewhere there remains the sacred that is distorted. In his distortions of the world man creates the tragic and the comic. We have seen how he can live better with the tragic by means of humor.

Y. *The Bible and Humor*

A playful sense of humor remains the key to unlocking some of the mysteries of the Bible. We dare not laugh at scripture as if *it* were funny. The book remains God's revelation to us! And that revelation reveals humor. (The previous section on revelation and humor can enlighten further this statement.)

The ontological examinations of humor contained in this book can help create a pattern for interpreting biblical passages with due regard for their own humor. Many people accept scripture on a far too pondersome and serious basis; the aura of sanctity obscures the true humanity of biblical personages, which includes their sense of humor. Humor is inherently a part of the finite makeup of men and women; indeed, they are human beings precisely in their playful humor.

Since human nature *is* to be playful-in-humor, (1) people must have been playful in the real-life Bible situation; (2) people must at some time have been playful-in-humor while writing scripture; and (3) people can be playful-in-humor as they interpret scripture now. This means the character in the Bible can interpret scripture humorously whether the writer of the scripture wrote humorously or not, or whether the reader can interpret scripture humorously. This means that the reader can interpret humorously whether the character in the story or the writer of the story was playful-in-humor or not—if Truth spotlights the incongruity for the reader.

The third genre is used in biblical exegesis when the ludicrous jumps out at us as we read the sagas and folk tales; for example, in the story of *Esther* Haman thinks the king is talking about him when the king mentions honoring a good man. Haman spells out how to honor such a man, and ends honoring his hated enemy Mordecai by exactly his own prescription. Later he is hanged on the gallows he had prepared for Mordecai.

In the second genre we must be open to the humorous intent of the writer. We must be open to the Bible's character humor in the first genre. When we consider how humor may be couched in figures of speech (hardly is it likely that humor used in figures of speech listed in Part I of the book are left out of a literary classic such as the *Holy Bible*), the humorous possibilities for interpretation of scripture are more real than any "straight" interpretation can provide. For instance, when Jesus said to the Pharisees, "You have such a *fine* way of rejecting the commandments of God,"[87] is this to be interpreted as hyperbole or "straight"?

The ludicrous may also be seen in riddles, and in Proverbs: "Like a gold ring in a swine's snout is a beautiful woman without discretion." [88]

In the understanding of this ontology of humor we exegete all scripture in the light of Truth. "God is love." (I John 4:8) There is no incongruity in that scripture—no humor. But when man acts as if he were God, inside or outside of scripture, Truth spotlights the incongruity and elicits the humor. This means that there *can be* humor within every character in the Bible. Except Christ, of course, who *is* the Truth that permits us to see the humor.

Peril comes for the Bible reader when he/she takes his/her serious self to the Bible and reads into the scripture his/her own serious nature. This eisegesis assumes that the reader possesses Truth. When the reader laughs with Truth at himself/herself, he/she experiences the spirit that exegetes scripture.

Z. *Eschatology and Humor*

Being-itself created the world *ex nihilo* (out of nothing) and *is* so long as we are conscious of its (our) existence. The world as we know it (as it *is* to us) continues as long as we are in it, and for it. To the extent that we are not *with it* for whatever reason, then *the world* is not to that extent. A dimension of the eschaton then is that the end was with us from the beginning and remains even as history goes forward. The nothing (which is the final end of creation) remains ever-present in creation. While non-being remains the end, creation could not be without non-being. This means that Being-itself controls non-being in creation, and through the end of creation. A part of that eschaton (the end) shows itself in the visualized conflict between non-being (the end that was with us from the beginning) and the oughtness that arises out of Being-itself. That visualized conflict is but another gap, an incongruity in man's nature—the condition for humor. This brings humor right up to the chronological end of the world. The end of the world really is the end of man. There may be some other world for other creatures, but, as far as man is concerned, when he no longer *is*, neither is his world. At that moment when man no longer *is*, neither will there be humor. All incongruities are in man. When man ceases to be, incongruities do too. In the end all the gaps close. Only sublime fulfillment remains for those beings who know intimately the truth of Being-itself that once in time spotlighted incongruities but now enlighten eternally all beings who are one in His Spirit.

POSTSCRIPT

This book does not answer the problem of humor. Rather it accepts that the problem is ontological and proceeds to describe the problem in metaphysical terms. While these may look like ontological arguments, they are in fact ontological understandings. The reader, upon reflection, senses the *givenness* of these writings. The writing is more contemplative than argumentative or reasonable by deduction or induction. The *One Who Is*, Being-itself, overwhelms all reasoning with Presence, Is-ness; and says, "Here, I *am*." In the presence of that Truth we are not as we ought to be. We do funny things to give the impression that we've got it all together.

Humor, like anything else on earth, remains indescribable. But we know enough about its ontological workings to know that it does not have a dynamic quality identification in the same manner as does love, faith, or hope. Rather it remains reaction within the human *being* (read as a verb, not a noun). Humor-produced ethos causes one *to be* strong as long as that ethos is grounded in love (faith, hope, courage, and all other derivative gifts of Being-itself). At the very heart of life lived out, then, is humor. Always active in its reaction to life's incongruities. Always ongoing. Never static. Humor is to be understood to the extent that we know we are to enjoy it. Not understood as an intellectualized object. It would be hell (non-being) if we did that. If we should think that by reading this book on humor that we have got an intellectual hold on the subject, we have set ourselves up as an unintended comic character. If by reading this book we open ourselves to Divine Truth, we may understand that in all times and all places on this earth incongruities exist, that "He who sits in the Heavens laughs" (Psalm 2:4)—and that we can too.

Notes

1. See Worcester, *The Art of Satire* (Cambridge: Harvard University Press, 1940); Johnson, *A Treasury of Satire* (New York: Simon and Schuster, 1945); Feinberg, *Introduction to Satire* (Ames: Iowa State University Press, 1967).
2. Marie Collins Swakey, *Comic Laughter* (New Haven: Yale University Press, 1961), pp. 12-13.
3. Max Eastman, *The Sense of Humor* (New York: Scribners, 1921), pp. 209-10.
4. Paul Tillich, *Systematic Theology,* Vol. III (Chicago: University of Chicago Press, 1963), p. 96.
5. Tillich, *Systematic Theology,* Vol. II (1957), pp. 50-51.
6. Dante, *The Divine Comedy,* translated by Lawrence Grant White (New York: Pantheon Books, 1948), p. 88.
7. *Ibid.,* p. 144.
8. Feinberg, *op. cit.,* p. 101.
9. Charles Davis, *God's Grace in History* (Fontana, 1966), p. 37.
10. Colin Morris, *Mankind My Church* (New York: Abingdon Press, 1971), p. 84.
11. Tillich, *op. cit.,* Vol. II, p. 49.
12. *Ibid.,* p. 31.
13. *Ibid.,* p. 63.
14. Romans 8:26-28.
15. S.I. Hayakawa, *Language in Thought and Action,* 3d ed. (New York: Harcourt Brace Jovanovich, 1972), pp. 258-9.
16. Tillich, *op. cit.,* Vol. I (1951), p. 168.
17. Dudley Zuver, *Salvation By Laughter* (New York: Harper, 1933), p. 89.
18. Tillich, *op. cit.,* Vol. II, p. 131.
19. *Loc. cit.*
20. *Ibid.,* pp. 143-4.
21. Jeremiah 20:8-9.
22. Romans 7:19-25.
23. Tillich, *op. cit.,* Vol. II, p. 22.
24. *Ibid.,* p. 42.
25. Max Eastman, *Enjoyment of Laughter* (New York: Simon & Schuster, 1936), p. 272.
26. *Ibid.,* p. 273.
27. Tillich, *op. cit.,* Vol. I, pp. 253-4.
28. *Ibid.,* p. 189.
29. Tillich, *op. cit.,* Vol. III, p. 94.
30. *Ibid.,* p. 94.
31. *Ibid.,* p. 93.
32. George Friedrich Meier, *Thoughts on Jesting* (Austin: University of Texas Press, 1947), p. 60.
33. *Ibid.,* p. 336.
34. Mark 7:9.

35. Matthew 23:24.
36. Soren Kierkegaard, *Concluding Unscientific Postscript* (Princeton University Press, 1941), p. 459.
37. Stephen Leacock, *Humor in Theory and Technique* (New York: Dodd, Mead, 1935), p. 15.
38. Swakey, *op. cit.*, p. 16.
39. Tillich, *op. cit.*, Vol. I, p. 267.
40. *Ibid.*, Vol. III, p. 48.
41. Peter L. Berger, *The Noise of Solemn Assemblies* (Garden City: Doubleday, 1961), p. 157.
42. Swakey, *op. cit.*, p. 14.
43. Victor Frankl, *Man's Search For Meaning* (New York: Washington Square Press, 1964), pp. 68-9.
44. Rollo May, *Paulus* (New York: Harper & Row, 1973), pp. 104-6.
45. Leacock, *op. cit.*, p. 268.
46. Eastman, *Enjoyment of Laughter*, p. 9.
47. *Ibid.*, p. 304.
48. Edward Corbett, *Classical Rhetoric For the Modern Student* (New York: Oxford University Press, 1971), pp. 459-95.
49. Julian N. Hartt, *The Restless Quest* (Philadelphia: Pilgrim Press, 1975), pp. 219-32.
50. *Ibid.*, pp. 128-9.
51. *Ibid.*, pp. 126-8.
52. Eastman, *op. cit.*, p. 41.
53. *Ibid.*, p. 42.
54. Tillich, *Dynamics of Faith* (New York: Harper & Row, 1957), p. 12.
55. *Ibid.*, p. 35.
56. *Ibid.*, p. 108.
57. Tillich, *The New Being* (New York: Charles Scribner's Sons, 1955), p. 38.
58. John 8:32.
59. Tillich, *The Shaking of The Foundations* (New York: Charles Scribner's Sons, 1948), p. 20.
60. *Ibid.*, p. 20.
61. Tillich, *Systematic Theology*, Vol. I, p. 189.
62. *Op. cit.*, Vol. III, p. 222.
63. *Ibid.*, p. 224.
64. *Ibid.*, p. 226.
65. Tillich, *The New Being*, p. 145.
66. Tillich, *Systematic Theology*, Vol. III, p. 274.
67. *Ibid.*, Vol. II, p. 58.
68. *Ibid.*, Vol. I, p. 284.
69. *Ibid.*, p. 201.
70. Tillich, *The Courage To Be* (New Haven: Yale University Press, 1952), p. 48.
71. *Loc. cit.*

72. *Ibid.*, p. 175.
73. Tillich, *Systematic Theology,* Vol. III, pp. 119-20.
74. *Ibid.*, Vol. I, p. 117.
75. *Ibid.*, p. 116.
76. *Ibid.*, Vol. II, p. 65.
77. Tillich, *Dynamics of Faith,* p. 34.
78. Tillich, *Systematic Theology,* Vol. III, p. 232.
79. *Ibid.*, Vol. I, p. 118.
80. *Ibid.*, p. 276.
81. John 8:32.
82. Tillich, *op. cit.,* Vol. III, p. 406.
83. *Ibid.*, p. 231.
84. *Ibid.,* p 232.
85. Tillich, *The Protestant Era* (Chicago: University of Chicago Press, 1948), p. 117.
86. Mircea Eliade, *The Sacred and the Profane: The Nature of Religion* (New York: Harcourt Brace), p. 64.
87. Mark 7:9.
88. Proverbs 11:22.

ONTOLOGY OF HUMOR
Bob W. Parrott

Foreword by Norman Vincent Peale

This book holds as its basic premise that humor functions in an ontological dimension which involves the intersection of truth with our everyday experiences and perceptions. The cracks in the walls of our ordinary life which let the light of truth seep through are the incongruities of our existence, gaps between what we are and what we ought to be. A glimpse of these gaps, afforded by the illumination of truth, triggers humor. When we see our incongruities as God sees them it is good humor; but without God's insight into our situation it becomes bad humor.

The ambiguity of what is and what is not lies within the being/non-being of humans, not in the being of God, who is Being-in-Itself. God in His mind sees incongruities in us and shares His insight with us by spotlighting with truth these incongruities. We can laugh because God does.

This book will serve to help those in many fields of human experience in thinking about some vital theological issues.